THE ORTHODOX BIBLE S
SERIES

The Epistle to the Romans: A Gospel for All

by Fr. Lawrence R. Farley

Conciliar Press
Ben Lomond, California

THE EPISTLE TO THE ROMANS:
A GOSPEL FOR ALL

one volume of *The Orthodox Bible Study Companion* Series

Published by Conciliar Press
P.O. Box 76
Ben Lomond, California 95005-0076

Printed in the United States of America

ISBN 1-888212-51-9

Dedicated to my wife, Donna,
who is the wind beneath my wings,
and the grace of God to me

Table of Contents and Outline

Introduction

A Word about Scholarship, Translation, and Format

This commentary was written for your grandmother. And for your plumber, your banker, your next-door neighbor, and the girl who serves you French fries at the nearby McDonald's. That is, it was written for the average layman, for the nonprofessional who feels a bit intimidated by the presence of copious footnotes, long bibliographies, and all those other things which so enrich the lives of academics. It is written for the pious Orthodox layman who is mystified by such things as Source Criticism, but who nonetheless wants to know what the Scriptures mean.

Therefore, it is unlike many other commentaries, which are written as contributions to the ongoing endeavor of scholarship and as parts of a continuous dialogue among scholars. That endeavor and dialogue is indeed worthwhile, but the present commentary forms no part of it. For this commentary assumes, without argument, a certain point of view, and asserts it without defense, believing it to be consistent with the presuppositions of the Fathers and therefore consistent with Orthodox Tradition. It has but one aim: to be the sort of book a busy parish priest might put in the hands of an interested parishioner who says to him over coffee hour after Liturgy, "Father, I'm not sure I really get what St. Paul is saying in the Epistles. What does it all mean?" This commentary tries to tell the perplexed parishioner what the writers of the New Testament mean.

Regarding the translation used herein, an Italian proverb says, "All translators are traitors." (The proverb proves its own point, for it sounds better in Italian!) The point of the proverb, of course, is that no translation, however careful, can bring out all the nuances and meanings of the original, since no language can be the mathematical equivalent of another. The English translator is faced, it would seem, with a choice: either he can make the translation something of a rough paraphrase of the original and render it into flowing sonorous English; or he can attempt to make a fairly literal, word-for-word translation from the original with the resultant English being stilted, wooden, and clumsy.

These two basic and different approaches to translation correspond to two basic and different activities in the Church. The Church needs a translation of the Scriptures for use in worship. This should be in good, grammatical, and flowing English, as elegant as possible and suited to its function in the majestic worship of the Liturgy. The Church also needs a translation of the Scriptures for private study and for group Bible study. Here the elegance of its English is of lesser concern. What is of greater concern here is the bringing out of all the nuances found in the original. Thus this approach will tend to sacrifice elegance for literality and, wherever possible, seek a word-for-word correspondence with the Greek. Also, because the student will want to see how the biblical authors use a particular word (especially St. Paul, who has many works included in the canon), a consistency of translation will be sought and the same Greek word will be translated, wherever possible, by the same English word or by its cognate.

The present work does not pretend to be anything other than a translation for private Bible study. It seeks to achieve, as much as possible, a literal, word-for-word correspondence with the Greek. The aim has been to present a translation from which one could jump back into the Greek original with the aid of an interlinear New Testament. Where a single Greek word has been used in the original, I have tried to find (or invent!) a single English word.

The result, of course, is a translation so literally rendered from the Greek that it represents an English spoken nowhere on the planet! That is, it represents a kind of "study Bible English" and not an actual vernacular. It was never intended for use outside the present commentaries, much less in the worship of the Church. The task of producing a flowing, elegant translation that nonetheless preserves the integrity and nuances of the original I cheerfully leave to hands more competent than mine.

A final word about the actual format of this work. In all these pages, the translated text is first presented in boldface type. Italics in this biblical text represent a word required by English syntax that is not actually present in the Greek.

The biblical text is followed by a commentary. In this commentary section, citations from the portion of text being commented upon are given in boldface type. Citations from other locations in Scripture are given in quotation marks with a reference; any reference not including a book name refers to the Book of Romans. In the commentary, italics are also used in the ordinary way—for emphasis, foreign words, etc.

Rome and the World

"The light of a new day was loosened with the rushing of eagles and the coming of the name," as G. K. Chesterton wrote in *The Everlasting Man*, "—the name that came with a thunderclap when the world awoke to Rome."

Not only is it difficult to understand much of the history of the early Church without knowing what Rome meant to the ancient world, it is difficult to understand much of history at all. In Chesterton's fine phrase, "the world awoke to Rome." That is, most men of the Mediterranean world came to think of Rome, a small town on the banks of the Tiber, as their own hometown. Rome belonged to everyone. It was international and cosmopolitan, the source of all law and order, the upholder of stability; the roads that led to it ran through the hearts of all men.

Well, almost all men. In the Roman world, there was one people who did *not* rejoice in Rome, but saw it as the great rival to God, a standing challenge and insult to the Most High. That people was Israel. For the Jews, Rome was not their city, but the stronghold of the enemy. They referred to it as Babylon (a practice taken over by the Christians, see 1 Pet. 5:13). The Jews considered it to be the source of all idolatry, debauchery, and uncleanness, the sinkhole of the world. It was the embodiment of all that existed outside the sacred confines of the land of Israel, the heart of the Gentile world of darkness.

We can see, then, why St. Paul felt compelled and eager to preach the Gospel also to those who were in Rome (1:15). The Gospel had traveled, as St. Luke tells us in his Acts of the Apostles, from Jerusalem to Rome, from its natural home in holy Israel to the heart of the Gentile world. There it had taken root, as a sign and promise that it would take root everywhere. For if the Gospel of peace and righteousness could survive and flourish in Rome, which had dedicated itself to war and hedonistic idolatry, it could survive and flourish anywhere.

That the Church had managed to establish itself in the city of Rome seemed to be a kind of miracle—and it meant that the Church could be established in *every* city. The existence of the church in Rome was a sign that Christianity no longer belonged to Israel alone, as one Jewish sect among many others. It was apparent to all now that the Church was destined to live in all the world, as the hope and soul of *all* men, both Jewish and Gentile. St. Paul felt the Lord's call deep in his apostolic heart to take the Gospel to every land, to all the places where Christ had not yet been named (15:20). How then could he not visit Rome also—the place and church whose very existence seemed to express his own calling? From Rome he could be sent even farther afield.

St. Paul and the Church of Rome

St. Paul did not found the Church of Rome. (Nor, it would seem, did St. Peter.) Rather, it seems to have been founded by now-nameless ordinary Christian believers, by men and women visiting Rome as merchants and soldiers, who took their faith and message with them wherever they went (see Acts 2:10).

The apostle wrote his Epistle to Rome from Corinth, in about the spring of the year 58. He had visited Corinth after a delay in passing through Macedonia. He had collected money from many churches in Macedonia and Achaia to give to the poor in Jerusalem—a project dear to his heart and one which would help unify the Church, binding Jew and Gentile together. His plan was to take this collection to Jerusalem and then to proceed to Rome, with a view to being helped by the Roman Christians on his way farther west—even, he hoped, to distant Spain.

St. Paul was, of course, never to fulfill this plan in the way he intended, for he was arrested in Jerusalem, and when he finally did visit Rome, it was as Caesar's prisoner, awaiting trial under house arrest. But all this lay in the future. At the time of writing, St. Paul's mind was bright with hopes of walking freely and boldly into the Roman capital, proclaiming to all the universal Gospel of Christ. The epistle was a part of the advance preparation for that visit.

For he had some work to do in Rome, as he had wherever he went. In Corinth, he had experienced much difficulty because his good name had been slandered and his apostolic authority denied by the Judaizers, his ever-present adversaries. These were Jews hailing from Jerusalem who opposed Paul, denying that he was an authentic apostle and insisting that Gentile Christians should be circumcised. They dogged Paul's steps and did all they could to blacken his reputation. With many Jews in the Roman Church, there were perhaps some there who had heard these rumors and wondered about this controversial man who was coming to them uninvited. Was his teaching truly unsound, as some had said? Should they welcome him? Should they support him and help him carry on his work farther afield?

In order to smooth the way for his visit, St. Paul writes this epistle to show the Roman Christians how orthodox his doctrine is. In so doing, he spends much time debating with his invisible Judaizing opponents and vindicating his universal understanding of the Gospel.

For the Judaizers had many objections. Paul should be ashamed to preach such things (1:16). For (the Judaizers said) he denied that the Jews had any advantage over the Gentiles at all and he denigrated circumcision as worthless (3:1). True, they admitted, some in Israel were faithless, rejecting Jesus—but Israel was still Israel! Paul was saying that God had cast off His ancient People whom He foreknew (9:6; 11:1, 2). That could never be: God must bless His chosen covenant People regardless of their sins. What mattered was circumcision—that they were still a part of His covenant (2:25f). Otherwise, what then shall we say about Abraham? To be his children meant to be circumcised (4:1f). That fellow Paul, with his insistence that all one needed to be saved was baptismal faith and dedication to Christ, was overthrowing everything. Why, if the Law and circumcision were no longer necessary for one to be justified and forgiven, that would lead to moral chaos! One might as well say that one should keep on sinning in order to have more forgiveness and grace (6:1f)!

It was in order to reply to these objections that St. Paul wrote his epistle. He wanted to set forth his understanding of the Gospel and answer his critics once and for all so that the Church at Rome would accept his authority and welcome him as an authentic apostle, supporting him and sending him away farther west, where he wanted to go. In writing this reply, he not only gave a lengthy and lucid explanation of the Gospel. He also gave an inspiring exhortation on how to live in love, as a mixed Christian community, coping with the inevitable tensions that would arise when those as different as Jew and Gentile lived closely together as one (as was the case in Rome).

The epistle was dictated to Tertius and sent by the hand of Phoebe, a rich patron of the church who lived in Cenchrea, next door to Corinth (16:1, 22). In sending it off to Rome, St. Paul committed his epistle to history as well, and it abides in the Church as a precious testament of the great Apostle to the Gentiles—the one who was eager to travel the road to Rome and to all the Gentile world.

I

OPENING
(1:1–15)

§I.1 Greetings

1 1 Paul, a slave of Jesus Christ, a called apostle,
separated for the Gospel of God
2 which He pre-promised through His prophets
in *the* Holy Scriptures,
3 concerning His Son, who came from the seed
of David according to the flesh
4 and was appointed Son of God in power according to *the* Spirit of holiness by His resurrection from *the* dead, Jesus Christ our Lord,
5 through whom we have received grace and apostleship for *the* obedience of faith among all the nations on behalf of His Name,
6 among whom also are you *yourselves*, the called
of Jesus Christ;
7 to all those who are in Rome, beloved of God, called *to be* saints: Grace to you and peace from our Father and the Lord Jesus Christ.

All ancient epistles began with the name of the sender, the name of the addressee, and a salutation. It could be as simple as "Apion to his father Epimachus: heartiest greetings." St. Paul usually let the Gospel message that filled his heart overflow from his lips, turning even this customary epistolary greeting into a kind of Christian blessing. Thus, all his epistles begin with a more fulsome assertion of his apostolic authority and a "double-barreled" blessing of grace and peace.

In his Epistle to the Romans, it seems that he is even more than usually anxious to convince his readers of his grasp of the Gospel message, and his opening greeting abounds even more. He describes himself as **a slave of Jesus Christ**—one who, like a slave, does nothing on his own authority, but always acts upon the orders of his Master—telling them that this epistle is in some sense written at the behest of the Lord and with His authority. This slavery is the essence of Paul's apostolate. As in all his epistles, he asserts his apostolic authority, saying that he was **called** to be an **apostle** when the Lord intervened in his life on the road to Damascus, overturning all his plans and bringing him from darkness to light. On that day he was **separated for the Gospel of God**. That is, God took him away from all his previous plans, from all the values and categories of this age, from all the powers of this world. Henceforth, Paul was to live only for the Lord, to spread His Holy Gospel.

Reference to **the Gospel of God**—the subject nearest Paul's heart and his reason for living—leads him to launch into an extended parenthesis, interrupting the normal flow of the opening greeting, as he describes this Gospel. His enthusiasm for the Gospel overflows the normal bounds of the conventions of letter-writing.

Thus he describes this Gospel as **pre-promised through His prophets in *the* Holy Scriptures**. That is, the Christian movement is no accident of history, no mere twist or turn in the ongoing development of Israel's existence. It is the culmination and goal of Israel's history and existence, the reason that Abraham was called, that the Patriarchs were given the land, that the Living God dwelt in the midst of His chosen People. In the Holy Scriptures of Israel, all of God's prophets and holy ones—prophetic men such as Moses, David, Isaiah, Jeremiah—spoke of this Gospel (see Matt. 27:9; John 12:41; Acts 2:30; 7:37). That is, in "many and various ways" (Heb. 1:1) the Kingdom of God was foretold. Some prescribed laws that had symbolic and typological significance, some wrote poetry that had application far beyond its day, some prophesied directly of the time the Lord would come and save Israel. Whether they knew it or not, all spoke of Jesus and the Gospel salvation He would bring. Thus, the Hebrew Scriptures were all prophetic, for they represented and pointed to a promise of God's future intervention. Paul's apostolic message is that this intervention has come in Jesus.

This Gospel that is the goal of Israel's history is **concerning His Son . . . Jesus Christ our Lord.** In saying this, St. Paul is not simply affirming the obvious. Rather, he is asserting that the Gospel provision for God's People centers on the Person of Jesus, not on the Law. It is Christocentric, not nomocentric (from the Gr. *nomos,* "law"). The Jews asserted that the Law was the standard by which all was judged and that it was ultimate and eternal, the context in which everything else found its subordinate place—including the Messiah. Paul, on the contrary, teaches that the Messiah, Christ our Lord, is the context into which everything else fits. The Law is not eternal, but was always meant to be superseded when the Messiah came. Thus, the eschatological Gospel is concerning God's Son, not the Law.

This Son is said to be proven to be the Messiah by the twofold and confirming witness of both history and God Himself, who is transcendent above history. What St. Paul is discussing here is not the two natures of Christ, divine and human. (Christ is indeed one Person in two natures, but that is not St. Paul's present concern.) The apostle is not discussing the *nature* of Christ, but the *witness* to Christ.

Thus he says that Jesus of Nazareth's status as Messiah is witnessed to by history—for He **came from the seed of David according to the flesh,** born of the proper historical lineage. The Messiah had to be born of David's seed and be his true and linear descendant in order to inherit the promises made to the House of David. That Jesus was indeed born from David's line, in his prophesied hometown of Bethlehem, witnesses to His being the Messiah (see Matt. 2:4–6).

Jesus' messianic status was also confirmed by God Himself, when He **appointed** Him **Son of God** by raising Him from the dead. By that act of **power** (Gr. *dunamis*—the same word used to designate a miracle, see 2 Cor. 12:12) God revealed Him to Israel as His true Messiah, raising Him **according to the Spirit of holiness**. God raised Jesus from the dead by His Spirit (8:11) as a supernatural act transcending all the powers of this historical age, exalting Him to His right hand so that henceforth Christ lives and reigns in the transcendence of the Kingdom of God. (The Spirit by which He was raised is called here the **Spirit of holiness**, instead of simply the "Holy Spirit," because He is the same Spirit whom we also receive and by whom we also are made holy.) Using the common Jewish terminology, St. Paul speaks of Jesus as being **appointed** Messiah through the act of resurrection, because by definition the Messiah is One who reigns in power, and it was through His Resurrection that He began that reign.

Thus, Jesus' status as Messiah is made doubly clear and sure, for He was revealed to be the Messiah both by genealogical history (**according to the flesh**) and also by the suprahistorical power of the resurrection (**according to *the* Spirit**).

It was through this Messiah that Paul received his own commission. Jesus was the One who appeared to him, giving him **grace** and forgiveness of his past sins, bestowing the gift and responsibility of **apostleship** upon him. This apostolic authority is not for Paul's own use and aggrandizement. He has a task to perform. His job as the Lord's slave is to go **among all the nations** and preach this Gospel so that all the Gentile nations might be brought to the **obedience of faith**. Formerly, as pagans, they lived in disobedience to God's Law and to righteousness, walking in idolatry, sensuality, and darkness. Now, as those having faith in the true God, they are to live in obedience to Him, becoming "[obedient] from the heart [to] that pattern of teaching to which [they] were delivered" (6:17).

This mandate to reach the nations includes the Romans themselves, who are also **called of Jesus Christ**. Even these, living in notorious and sinful Rome, are called by the Lord and now belong to Him. Thus, the apostle's mandate is to preach to them too. He is to strive to make all nations obedient to the faith, so that his sacrificial offering of the Gentiles to God might be acceptable (15:16). How then can he not visit the Romans as well—for this is also a part of his apostolic commission. That is why he is writing now **to all those who are in Rome.** They too are **beloved of God**, as true Christians, and share the Gospel call to be **saints**, sharing God's own holiness. As one who has been told to minister to all the nations, he has no choice but to minister to those in Rome as well.

§I.2 Thanksgiving for the opportunity to preach the Gospel in Rome

8 First, I give thanks to my God through Jesus
Christ for all of you, because your faith is proclaimed in all the world.
9 For God is my witness, whom I worship in my
spirit in the Gospel of His Son, how unceasingly I make remembrance of you,
10 always beseeching in my prayers, if perhaps
now at last by the will of God I may be pros-
pered to come to you.
11 For I long to see you that I may impart some
spiritual gift to you, so that you may be established;
12 that is, that I may be coencouraged *while*
among you, through one another's faith, both
yours and mine.
13 And I do not want you to be ignorant, brothers, that often I have planned to come to you
(and was hindered until the present), that I
might have some fruit among you also, even as
among the rest of the Gentiles.
14 I am a debtor both to Greeks and to barbarians, both to the wise and to the mindless.
15 Thus as for me, *I am* ready to preach *the Gospel* to you also who are in Rome.

As of **first** importance, in the customary epistolary thanksgiving, St. Paul **gives thanks to** his **God** for the great **faith** and piety of the Romans. So great is his gratitude for their faith that he offers his prayer **through Jesus Christ**, like a solemn liturgical eucharist. That is, he is not casually expressing a mere wish, but making a deliberate act of thanksgiving and praise for their piety. For their piety is so exemplary that it is **proclaimed in all the world**. Just as the faith and trials of those in Thessalonica have become proverbial (see 1 Thess. 1:6–8), so has the faith of those in Rome achieved far-flung fame. (This was a sign of the international stature Rome was later to acquire in the Church.) It is because of this greatness and faith that St. Paul longs to visit them.

They must not assume, he assures them, that his not having visited them is a sign of his indifference. Far from it! Rather, as he calls **God** to be his **witness** in a solemn oath, he has often wanted to come. As surely as he **worship**s God in his **spirit** and serves him in the integrity of his secret heart through his preaching of **the Gospel of His Son**, he has wanted to make the visit. The word translated here as *worship* is the Greek *latreuo*, which is the word used for serving at the altar in sacrificial worship (see Heb. 9:9). By using this word, St. Paul refers to his apostolic preaching ministry to the Gentiles, in which he offers them as an acceptable sacrifice to God (15:16). He is saying that he longs to include the Romans in his apostolic ministry of offering the Gentiles to God. Thus he **unceasingly makes remembrance of** them and **beseech**es God in his **prayers** that He would allow Paul to come to them.

He is determined that they not **be ignorant** of how he longs to visit them and how he would have come before now, but has been **hindered until the present** by the multitude of his trials and adventures. And he wants to come, not to take from them, but rather to *give* something to them. He longs to **impart some spiritual gift** to them. What is this spiritual gift (Gr. *charisma pneumatikon*)? Paul may intend some apostolic gift of healing or miracle, but it is more likely that he refers to a gift of teaching, revelation, or prophecy. For the result of the gift will be that they are **established** and strengthened and made more stable in their faith. Also, he speaks of their being **coencouraged** (Gr. *sumparakaleo*), and one of the functions of teaching and prophecy was encouragement (Gr. *paraklesis*, 1 Cor. 14:3). So it seems most likely that he wants to come to teach them, to build them up in the faith and lead them to greater maturity and stability.

With his customary humility, he immediately adds that this establishing of their faith through his visit is a matter of *mutual* benefit—that he will benefit from them as much as they from him. He hastens to assure them that he will be **coencouraged** ***while*** **among** them. Just as they will be encouraged by his teaching, so he will be encouraged by their faith.

He has long planned to come and see them, that he might **have some fruit** from them also, just as he has from **among the rest of the Gentiles**. He has visited everywhere else and has been encouraged by the believers' faith, benefiting spiritually from his time among them. He wants to do the same in Rome. Indeed, he is **a debtor** and under obligation to do so! For Christ has laid upon him the obligation to **preach** the Gospel to absolutely everyone—both to the cultured **Greeks** and the uncultured **barbarians**, both to the philosophically **wise** and to the unreflective **mindless**. Since he has such a mandate to preach the Gospel to all people of the earth, whatever their state, he of course is **ready** to do so to those also **who are in Rome**. With such a universal mandate, how could he omit such an important place as the capital of the world?

Notes for Section I:

Notes for Section I:

ꕥ II ꕥ

THE UNIVERSAL GOSPEL ST. PAUL WILL PREACH IN ROME (1:16—8:39)

St. Paul now begins to present the Gospel that he will preach in Rome. In doing this, he seeks not only to vindicate his apostolic authority by undercutting and refuting the Judaizers, who would deny that authority; he also seeks to impress his hearers with the depth of his knowledge of the Gospel, and so secure a warm welcome for himself when he comes.

The Judaizers (his unseen opponents throughout this Epistle) tend to limit the Gospel to its original Jewish context. It is not, they say, that Gentiles should not be converted to Christ. It is rather that Gentiles, once converted to Christ, should become circumcised and thus become Jews. Gentiles *as Gentiles* cannot, they feel, stand on the same level as Jewish believers in the Messiah. The Jews, as the People of God, marked by the divinely given covenant of circumcision, have a superiority to the Gentiles. Any Gentile disciple of Jesus, they insist, should be properly circumcised. Paul, with his insistence on the complete irrelevance of circumcision, seems to them to threaten the whole Jewish context of the Gospel, and thus to overthrow the covenant of God.

In answering these Judaizers, St. Paul strives to show how the Gospel is offered equally and on the same terms to both Gentile and Jew—that is, it is offered on the basis on faith. Faith in Christ—expressed in Holy Baptism, manifested in a life of holiness in the Church—is all that God asks. This faith and discipleship to Jesus do not need, as the Judaizers assert, to be supplemented by circumcision. The obedience of faith is enough. Anyone who gives his life unreservedly to Jesus, serving Him in righteousness and penitence, can be assured of His forgiveness and salvation. Thus Paul argues that the same Gospel, with its provision of salvation by faith, is presented to Jew and Gentile alike. The Gentile is saved by faith (without circumcision)—and the Jew too is saved by faith (with circumcision being completely superfluous). This is entirely fitting, because both Jew and Gentile are equally held in the power of sin: the same remedy is given to both, because both suffer from the same disease.

Sin is universal. It binds all the nations of the earth, stopping their mouths and leaving them without defense before God. It binds all in Israel too, leaving the Jews equally without defense. God hates sin in *all*—the Jews do not have any sort of immunity from divine censure because they are circumcised. If they sin, they are guilty, just as the uncircumcised Gentiles are. Both Jew and Gentile are in the same situation. Sin is judged in both—just as righteousness is rewarded in both. And as both are struck with the same affliction, so both are offered the same way of healing—justification and vindication by faith. If any man—Jew or Gentile—will but embrace Jesus Christ and follow Him as His true disciple, this man will be saved. Circumcision, Jewishness, and nationality play no part in salvation. The penitent man emerges from the waters of baptism washed, sanctified, and justified (see 1 Cor. 6:11). All he needs is faith. The one who has "faith in Christ Jesus" and who is "baptized into Him" can rest assured that he has "clothed himself with Christ." In that salvation, there is "neither Jew nor Greek" (see Gal. 3:26–28). It is this universal Gospel that Paul is going to proclaim in Rome—a Gospel for all men.

§II.1 The Gospel universal in scope because sin is universal

1 **16 For I am not at all ashamed of the Gospel, for**
it is the power of God for salvation to every-
one who has faith, to the Jew first and also to
the Greek.
17 For in it *the* righteousness of God is revealed

by faith to faith, as it is written, "The righteous shall live by faith."

Having said that he is ready and eager to preach the Gospel in Rome when he comes, St. Paul declares that he is indeed **not *at all* ashamed** of that Gospel. The word translated here *at all ashamed* is the Greek *epaischunomai,* which differs a bit from the verb "to be ashamed" (Gr. *aischuno*) in that it seems to be a more intensive form (hence the addition here of the English *at all*). St. Paul's Judaizing detractors intimate that Paul should indeed be ashamed of his message, since it overthrows (as they think) the Abrahamic covenant of God, denying the necessity of circumcision. But Paul is utterly unabashed and bold. He is not ashamed of his message—for whoever receives it experiences the **power of God for salvation**. The proof of the validity of his message is in the changed lives of those who receive it! Thus he boldly offers it to all—**to the Jew first**, since the Jew has the ancient covenantal right to the Messiah. St. Paul never denies this historical Jewish foundation of the faith. Whenever he enters a new town, he first preaches in the Jewish synagogues, giving Israel the first chance to receive their promised Messiah. But he offers it **also to the Greek** or Gentile. For Christ came powerfully to save all the children of men.

In this Gospel, ***the*** **righteousness of God is revealed** and manifestly experienced as being **by faith to faith**—that is, as experienced through faith throughout. Circumcision and other works of the Jewish Law have no part here. The transfiguring power of God works in one's life as one walks by faith, loving Christ, serving Him, trusting His mercy alone.

By the words ***the*** **righteousness of God**, St. Paul does not allude simply to God's judicial justice—to His ethical standards and His just judgment on sin. This is a part of it, but by no means the main part. In the terminology of the time, the term *righteousness* (Gr. *dikaiosune*) means all of God's love and perfection—His clemency and moderation, His forgiving heart and philanthropic beneficence. In Psalm 144:7 (LXX), it is a synonym for His kindness; in the Prophets (e.g. Is. 62:1 LXX), it is a parallel with His salvation. By

God's righteousness, St. Paul means all of God's abundant kindness and saving love. He means that all His lavish forgiving heart is revealed and experienced by those who will approach Him. And this approach is entirely, he asserts, a matter of faith and trust.

In typical fashion, he seals this assertion with a citation of Old Testament Scripture. As the Prophet Habakkuk said, **"The righteous shall live by faith"** (Hab. 2:4). The righteous man, Paul seems to say, is righteous because he has experienced the righteousness and mercy of God. It is through this experience that he will live and be rescued and prosper. And this is all because that righteous man walks by faith, serving the Lord in faithfulness and love. What God wants is that faithful heart. If one has that faith, that heart relationship with Him, one will live and know His blessing. Thus, the apostle says, his message is nothing else but what was proclaimed by Israel's ancestral faith. He proclaims salvation by faith—just as the Scriptures say.

18 For revealed is *the* wrath of God from heaven
against all impiety and unrighteousness of men,
who hold back the truth by unrighteousness,
19 because that which is known about God is
manifest among them, for God manifested *it*
to them.
20 For since the creation of *the* world, His unseen
***things* (*namely*, His everlasting power and di-**
vinity) have been *clearly* seen, being understood
through *the things* that have been made, so that
they are without defense.
21 For having known God, they did not glorify
***Him* as God or *give* thanksgiving, but they be-**
came useless in their questionings, and their
uninsightful heart was darkened.
22 Claiming to be wise, they became foolish,
23 and changed the glory of the incorruptible God

into a likeness of an image of corruptible man and of birds and quadrupeds and reptiles.

St. Paul now opens his long argument for the universality of the Gospel and for one and the same salvation being offered to all men, both Jew and Gentile. He shows how all the world stands guilty before God, turning his attention first to the Gentile world.

God's love and universal righteousness find their counterbalance in His universal **wrath**—as the former is revealed in the Gospel (v. 17), so is the latter **revealed** from His very throne, coming powerfully and directly **from heaven**. (The parallelism of the two revelations is expressed by stressing that His wrath is revealed just as His righteousness is—the word *revealed* in v. 18 is stressed by being placed at the beginning of the sentence in the Greek.) The transcendent and heavenly God reveals His judgment upon **men** on earth, judging them for all their **impiety** and idolatry and for all their **unrighteousness** and sinful behavior. He judges them in wrath, not merely because they are bad, but because they *personally reject Him*. Sin is not simply misbehaving; it is a deliberate repudiation of God and a refusal to know Him. It is the breaking off of a relationship, a personal rejection of the Most High. That is, all men—all the Gentiles, all the nations—know the truth about God, but they **hold back** or suppress that knowledge, turning from that truth to a life of unrighteousness and callous hardheartedness. They deliberately try to forget what they know, distracting themselves with a life of sin.

How do they have this knowledge of the truth? This truth is **manifest among them** and can be found in their midst, because **God manifested *it* to them**. That is, He manifested the truth that He is different from anything on earth, different from all their idols. All on earth is weak and transitory, but God is of **everlasting power**. All on earth is visible and physical, but God's nature is not; His is the true and bodiless **divinity**, transcendent above all. This fundamental truth has been revealed to them **since the creation of *the* world**—it is not a recent and advanced lesson for the elite, but a basic truth, which could always have been learned by any. The

unseen ***things*** of God's eternal and transcendent nature are thus ***clearly*** **seen** by them. The truth about the invisible God is visible to their mind's eye, **being understood through** ***the things*** **that have been made**. That is, as they contemplate the created world around them, they can know that God is not like that—that He is transcendent, greater than all the world. Even as an artist is greater than his artistic handiwork, so is the Creator greater than His creation.

Thus, they are **without defense**, utterly defenseless before His indictment. They know the divine nature is eternal and invisible, yet they turn to idols anyway, pushing away the truth about God that He has shown them through His creation. Instead of **glorifying** Him **as God** by offering **thanksgiving** (Gr. *eucharisto*), they plunge into **questionings** and philosophical disputes, becoming **useless** and unfit for anything good. In their inner hearts, there is no insight, no intelligence, no shrewdness or comprehension. For all the claims of the pagan philosophers to have wisdom, in their hearts there is nothing but darkness. No light of insight can be expected from them. They may trumpet their claim to be **wise**—but as idolaters, they are **foolish** and have nothing to offer.

Who can deny this? They know **the glory of the incorruptible God**—that He is eternal, unfading, glorious in His transcendence. But look at paganism now! They have been stupid enough to change the **glory** they could have had into the **likeness of an image of corruptible man**. In all the pagan temples of the world are those statues, all proclaiming that the divine nature is like the visible creation. They could have God, but they have chosen man; they could have the incorruptible, but they have chosen the corruptible. And not only do they say that God is like man—there are also statues of the gods in the image of **birds**—a lower form than man. And **quadrupeds**, which walk in lowliness on all fours—and even **reptiles**, the lowest order, which crawl on the earth! How can anyone imagine that paganism is anything but senselessness and insanity? Surely, the nations of the earth stand guilty before God, choosing such idols over the God they once knew.

24 Therefore God delivered them in the desires
of their hearts to uncleanness, that their bodies might be dishonored among them.
25 For they exchanged the truth of God for the
lie and reverenced and worshipped the creature beyond Him who created *it*, who is blessed
to the ages. Amen.
26 Because of this God delivered them over to
passions of dishonor, for their females exchanged the natural use for that which is
against nature,
27 and likewise also the males left the natural use
of the female and were burning up in their longing towards one another, males with males
working out the improper *thing* and receiving
in themselves the recompense of their error,
which was fit.
28 And just as they did not approve to have God
in real-knowledge, God delivered them to an
unapproved mind, to do the things which are
not proper,
29 being filled with all unrighteousness—evil,
greed, malice, full of envy, murder, strife, guile,
malignity—*they are* whisperers,
30 evil-speakers, God-haters, abusive, arrogant,
boastful, inventors of evil, unobedient to parents,
31 uninsightful, untrustworthy, unloving, unmerciful,
32 and, although they really-know the ordinance
of God, that those who practice such things
are worthy of death, they not only do the same,
but also *give* consent to those who practice
them.

God's wrath and judgment are revealed from His very throne. In what does this judgment consist? In being abandoned by God. That is, He **delivered** them up to their own sins (Gr. *paradokeo*—the same word used for delivering a tradition), that they might know by experience how bitter it is to forsake the Lord their God (see Jer. 2:19) and to live in a world from which God has been banished.

St. Paul stresses time and again here that this abandonment is caused by their fundamental and inner idolatry. They reject God, so He justly rejects them. They **exchanged the truth of God**—that He is invisible, eternal, transcendent above the creation—for **the lie.** Note the definite article—Greek *to pseudei*. By *the lie,* the apostle means "the idol." (See Isaiah 44:20 LXX, "[The idolater] will not say, 'Is there not a lie [i.e. an idol] in my right hand?'") Thus all in the pagan world **reverenced and worshipped the creature**, perversely giving honor and adoration to what has been created, wood and stone, rather than to **Him who created *it***, the eternal God who alone is worthy to be **blessed to the ages.** (The apostle, as a good Jew, adds his own liturgical **Amen** to this blessing of God.)

In using the word *delivered* three times in this passage (vv. 24, 26, 28), St. Paul seems to describe a threefold descent of the Gentile world into a maelstrom of moral chaos. For their idolatry and rejection of Him, God **delivered them in the desires of their hearts to uncleanness**. The word translated here *uncleanness* is the Greek *akatharsia*, usually used by the apostle to denote sexual uncleanness. St. Paul refers here to the sexual license that pervades the pagan world, so that the very **bodies** of persons, though made in the image of God, **might be dishonored among them.** That is, through the desires and lusts rooted deep in their hearts, everyone is viewed simply as an object to be used. Human bodies, made by God, are bought and sold for sex, like any other commodity, and thus are dishonored. Human flesh is intrinsically holy, but pagan society has sacrilegiously devalued it.

More than this (and as a further stage in their descent into depravity), God **delivered them over to passions of dishonor**. With a certain delicate reticence, the apostle here describes the homosexuality rampant in pagan culture. In the pagan society of his day, this homosexuality was often expressed in the commercial use of little boys (pederasty), a feature of certain debauched orgies. But it was expressed in consensual adult liaisons also. There is little doubt that St. Paul, educated according to the strictest sect of his religion (Acts 26:5), would categorically reject *all* homosexual activity (see Lev. 18:22). For him, only unions of male with female constitute **the natural use** decreed by God. Anything else is perversion, **against nature.** Once pagan society has banished knowledge of the true God, as a judgment God consigns them to their own passions. It is the way of fallen passions to follow a certain fatal progression, going from bad to worse, increasing in ferocity and perversity. (This is clearly seen by modern sex-addiction therapists.) Thus, fallen passions become ever more twisted and sick, and the one abandoned to his desires descends to ever-lower levels.

As an example of such low perversity, St. Paul relates that even **their females**—normally not given over to lust in the same way as men—have reached such depths. Thus lesbianism is, in the thought of the apostle (and the Church), not a valid "alternative lifestyle," but a sign of sickness in the society that approves it and of the judgment of God upon that society.

In this, the females are the counterbalance in sin to **the males**, who in homosexual passion **were burning up in their longing towards one another**. (The word translated here *burning up* is the Greek *ekkaio*—an intensive form of the normal word for "burning," *kauo*. The apostle thus describes not mere sexual passion, but passion burning out of control.) With a delicacy and reserve, he describes their homosexual act simply as **the improper *thing*** (Gr. *asxemosune*; see its use in 1 Cor. 12:23)—and the social diseases following it as **the recompense of their error, which was fit**. He seems reluctant to discuss such things.

In all this discussion, it is significant that St. Paul does not use the normal terms for man and woman, the Greek *aner* and *gunes*. Rather, he uses the terms for *male* and *female* (Gr. *arsen* and *thelus*), denoting gender in its more purely biological aspect. (Compare the cognate verb *thelazo* for the woman, meaning "to breastfeed.")

For when sin erodes the human person, gender is reduced to mere animal sexuality. Men cease to be men and become merely male; women are no longer true women, but simply female. Contrary to what secular image-makers may tell us, *real* men are holy, and a real woman is one who has embraced the way of sanctity.

As the final step down into complete moral chaos, St. Paul says that God **delivered them to an unapproved mind**. The apostle here makes a play on words not easily recaptured in English. He says that because pagan society **did not approve** (Gr. *dokimazo*) **to have God in real-knowledge**, He abandoned them to an **unapproved** (Gr. *adokimos*) mind. That is, He abandoned them to a mind which is utterly worthless, completely worthy of rejection. They have been called to have true and accurate knowledge of the living God (not just "knowledge"—Gr. *gnosis*, but *real-knowledge*—Gr. *epignosis*), but they deliberately push such saving knowledge away. Therefore God has withdrawn from them, allowing them **to do the things which are not proper**. Society has become a teeming mass of **unrighteousness**. Men's lives are dominated by **evil, greed, malice** as they prey viciously upon one another. They are **full of envy**, plotting **murder** against those they hate, quarrelling in **strife**, warring with **guile** and deceit, brooding with inner **malignity**, delighting to think the worst. They are **whisperers** (Gr. *psithuristas*—an onomatopoetic word) and backbiters; they are **evil-speakers** and slanderers. They are **God-haters**, opposing any form of restraint, law, or piety. They are **abusive** and insolent, lashing out in verbal cruelty; they are **arrogant** show-offs, **boastful** braggarts, **inventors of evil**, ever fertile in imagining schemes to snare the unwary.

They are **unobedient to parents, uninsightful, untrustworthy, unloving, unmerciful**. St. Paul here uses a series of five words, all beginning with the so-called alpha-privative—the *a-* prefix, which acts as a negative, like our English prefix *un-*. The list thus reads like a rapidly fired staccato of denunciations—*goneusin apeitheis, asunetous, asunthetous, astorgous, aneleemonas*—the repeated initial *a* sound making for greater emphasis. He is describing the pagan darkness which he sees reigning everywhere. Men are **unobedient** to parents (phrased this way, instead of the usual "disobedient," to conform to the sound of the words that follow). That is, they pursue their own pleasures, caring nothing for duties to parents. They are **uninsightful**, having no moral comprehension or discernment, unable to distinguish right from wrong. They are **untrustworthy** and unstable, lying whenever they think they need to. They are **unloving**, lacking in the Greek *storge*, the natural affection of parent for child. Thus they easily practice abortion and infanticide, coldly destroying their offspring in defiance of the natural bonds of parental love. They are **unmerciful** and pitiless, punishing and beating their slaves for a mere trifle.

In all the above, St. Paul paints a picture of a society gone mad, estranged from truth, turbulent with evil, sick with strife. It is a portrait of the Gentile world of his day (and our day!)—a world entirely darkened because it has extinguished the light given it by God.

And it is a world that has no excuse for its guilt. For they **really-know** and inwardly recognize the **ordinance of God**, their conscience bearing witness to them that such ways are evil and that **those who practice such things** are truly **worthy of death**. When others do it to them, they quickly condemn them to such a death in their inner hearts. Nonetheless, they still continue to **do the same** to others themselves. And not only that, but they also ***give* consent** and hearty approval to those others who practice them—all the better to justify themselves, when *they* practice them! Thus is the wrath of God revealed to men. The whole Gentile world is caught in a web of sin and guilt before God.

§II.2 As sin is judged in all, so righteousness will be rewarded in all—even in Gentiles

St. Paul continues his argument, making his case that the same Gospel is fitly offered to all, both Jew and Gentile. He has argued that this is fit because all the world is afflicted with the same malady of sin. Here he takes the next step. As all the world lies in sin, so all people will be judged for their sin—and also rewarded for their righteousness. One single moral standard applies to all, both Jew and Gentile. Thus it is fitting that one single Gospel apply to all, both Jew and Gentile—the Gospel of faith.

2 1 **Therefore you are without defense, O man, everyone who judges, for in that you judge the other, you condemn yourself, for you who judge practice the same things.**

2 **And we know that the judgment of God is according to truth against those who practice such things.**

3 **And do you reckon this, O man who judge those who practice such things and do the same, that you will flee-away from the judgment of God?**

4 **Or the riches of His kindness and the clemency and the patience do you despise, ignorant that the kindness of God leads you to repentance?**

5 **But because of your hardness and unrepentant heart you are treasuring up wrath for yourself in a Day of wrath and revelation of the righteous-judgment of God,**

The apostle continues from the thought of 1:32, where he said that the Gentiles are culpable because they do the same things they condemn in others. It is because of this that they are **without defense**—every single man of them who thus **judges** his neighbor while **practicing the same things**. In using the vocative **O man**, St. Paul means not only to emphasize that he addresses every single one of those who judge; he also means to call them to humility and to the realization that we are but men—weak, puny, transient (see the designation "son of man" in Hebrew, e.g. Ezek. 2:1).

He thus calls the unrighteous world to repentance. For he says that all **know that the judgment of God** and His divine case against sinners (Gr. *krima*; see its use in 1 Cor. 6:7) will be **according to truth.** That is, it will be just and incorruptible, condemning the guilty as they deserve. If they do the same as those sinners, do they **reckon** and count on being able to **flee-away** (not just "to flee"—Gr. *pheugo*, but "to flee clean away"—*ekpheugo*) and escape altogether that divine lawsuit against the unrighteous? They anticipate God's sentence on sinners whom they themselves condemn—that is, upon those sinners who hurt them. Will they themselves escape? Certainly not! To count on escaping His judgment is to **despise** and **devalue the riches of His kindness and the clemency and the patience** (placed at the beginning of the sentence in the Greek for emphasis).

For every day, God delays His judgment on the world, displaying how abundantly kind and mild He is, how clement and forbearing, how patient and longsuffering. This delay is meant to **lead to repentance**, inducing the thoughtful to repent and change their life. As one reflects on how good God is to withhold His wrath, one is called to repent. God's unfailing goodness is poured upon the world—the sun and rain upon the just and the unjust—as a summons to come home. Are the impenitent **ignorant** of this? If they continue to practice sin with **unrepentant heart**, heedless of the coming judgment—if they continue in **hardness** and unbending stubbornness (Gr. *skleroteta*; see the English "sclerosis" or hardening of the arteries)—they will simply be **treasuring up wrath** for themselves, which will break upon them in the final **Day of wrath.** They will not succeed in fleeing-away from the sentence of God. Having been stored up throughout the days of delay God has given them, it will catch up with them on the Last Day, when **the righteous-judgment of God** will be revealed.

6 **who will render to each according to his works—**
7 **to those who by perseverance of good work seek**
for glory and honor and incorruption, eternal
life,

8 but to those who are opportunistic and who
disobey the truth, but obey unrighteousness,
wrath and indignation.
9 *There will be* tribulation and anguish upon
every soul of man who works out wickedness,
of the Jew first and also of the Greek,
10 but glory and honor and peace to everyone who
works out the good, to the Jew first and also to
the Greek,
11 for there is no respect of persons with God.
12 For as many who have sinned lawlessly will
also be destroyed lawlessly, and as many who
have sinned in the Law will be judged through
the Law,
13 for not the hearers of the Law are righteous
with God, but the doers of the Law will be
justified.

For the Day of the Second Coming will be a time to reveal God's "righteous-judgment" (v. 5; Gr. *dikaiokrisia*). That is, it will reveal that God truly is righteous and that there are unshakable moral foundations to the world. In this age, one can deny this, for it seems that the victory is always to the strong and ruthless, that falsehood is ever on the throne and truth on the gallows. Righteousness often goes unrewarded, and unscrupulous men prosper. It would be easy for the cynical to conclude that there is no justice and that all is relative. But in the Age to Come, the truth will be revealed. Then all will know that righteousness is rewarded and unrighteousness punished, and that God is truly just.

For He will then **render to each according to his works**. That is, to those righteous who persevere in **good work**, being pious, kind, and just, because in the afterlife they **seek for glory and honor and incorruption**—to all such God will give **eternal life**. And to those unrighteous who were **opportunistic**, who unscrupulously clawed their way to the top, **disobeying the truth** of love for God and man, obeying instead **unrighteousness**—to all such God will render **wrath and indignation** in eternal punishment.

Indeed, there will be the **tribulation** of suffering and the **anguish** of eternal confinement and distress (Gr. *stenochsoria*—see its cognate in 2 Cor. 4:8, where the thought is one of being crushed under a weight) for **every** single **soul** and person who does evil—regardless of race or religion. Both **the Jew and also the Greek** will suffer the same judgment and the same fate if they **work out** the same **wickedness**. And in the same way, there will be **glory and honor and peace** in the Age to Come for **everyone** who does righteousness—regardless of race or religion. **The Jew first** will be judged, as being given the more complete revelation of God's eternal and visible nature and His righteous will. Then **the Greek** or Gentile will be judged too, as knowing these same truths through the things God has made (see 1:20). If the Greek **works out the good**, striving to serve God and do His will according to the light given him, he too will receive the same reward, because **there is no respect of persons with God**. That is, God does not measure the Jew with any different moral yardstick than He does the Gentile, nor grant any special immunity from judgment. The same standards, the same judgment, the same rewards apply equally to all.

The Gentiles who have **sinned lawlessly** (Gr. *anomos*), without reference to the Jewish Law, will **be destroyed lawlessly**, without reference to that Law. The Jews who **sinned in the Law**, transgressing what God had forbidden in the Mosaic Law, will **be judged through the Law**, suffering for its violation. What will matter on that Judgment Day is not hearing the Law read in synagogue or being part of the Jewish nation. What will matter, what will justify and lead to life "on a Day when God will judge the hidden things of men through Christ Jesus" (v. 16), is actually *doing* the Law.

---

14 (For when Gentiles not having *the* Law do
by nature the things of the Law, these, not
having the Law, are a Law to themselves,
15 in that they demonstrate the work of the Law

written in their hearts, their conscience co-witnessing and their reasonings alternatively accusing or else defending themselves)
16 on a Day when, according to my Gospel, God
will judge the hidden *things* of men through Christ Jesus.

Here those with Jewish background have a question, for the whole concept of moral compass is for them bound up with the Law. How then can the Gentiles, who do not have the Jewish Law, still persevere in good works and "work out the good" (v. 10)? How can the lawless Gentiles ever be "doers of the Law" (v. 13)?

St. Paul responds to this with a parenthesis, comprising verses 14 and 15. The Gentiles may not have the Jewish Law. Nonetheless, they can **do by nature** and instinctively (Gr. *phusei*) **the things of the Law**, practicing the piety, justice, and compassion the Law enjoins. Thus, even **not having the Law**, they still are **a Law to themselves** in the sense that their inner heart and conscience constitute their own version of the Jewish Law.

For it is possible for Gentiles, observing the glories of creation, to have inner heart knowledge of the glorious Creator and to strive to serve Him. The virtues of these righteous Gentiles **demonstrate** that the values and **work of the Law** are **written in their hearts**. The existence of this inner moral compass (as God's natural Law in the hearts of the Gentiles) is proven by the fact that their **conscience** acts as **cowitness** (Gr. *sum-marturouses*), witnessing along with their deeds. Their righteous deeds witness to such an inner Law within them, and so does their conscience—their **reasonings** sometimes **accusing** them (when they sin) or **defending** them (when they act rightly). The verdicts of this inner tribunal of the conscience prove that they are not without a true moral compass, and it is this inward and spontaneous instinct that acts for them as the Law does for the Jews.

17 But if you are *called* on by the name "Jew" and rest upon the Law and boast in God,
18 and know the will and approve the things that differ, being instructed out of the Law,
19 and are persuaded that you yourself are a guide of the blind ones, a light of those who are in darkness,
20 a disciplinarian of *the* senseless ones, a teacher of infants, having in the Law the form of the knowledge and of the truth—

St. Paul begins to close his first argument, making the case that as sin is judged in all (regardless of whether or not one is circumcised), so will righteousness be rewarded in all. He has shown that all the world is under sin and is guilty. He has shown that all will be judged according to the same standard, whether Jew or Gentile. Now he strives to show that circumcision (the badge of the Jew) is irrelevant to this process. The Gentiles, though physically uncircumcised, may still inherit the same reward as the circumcised Jews.

St. Paul begins making his case by addressing the Jew, calling him forward as a reluctant witness. The Jews are proud of their superiority over the Gentiles, for the Gentile wanders in moral darkness, whereas the Jew lives and basks in the divine light of the Law. He is ***called* on by the name "Jew"** proudly, as a badge of honor, **resting** and relying **upon the Law** (Gr. *epanapauomai*; see the related word *anapauo*, "to refresh"), taking comfort and support from it. He **boasts** that he knows God and **the will** of God—unlike the Gentile, who has no idea of what God wants. That is because he has been **instructed out of the Law**, so that he can **approve the things that differ**, distinguishing the true from the false, the morally precious from the worthless. Thus the Jew is **persuaded** that he is **a guide of the blind ones, a light of those who are in darkness, a disciplinarian of *the* senseless ones, a teacher of infants** who need instruction. For he possesses for himself **the Law**—the very **form** and embodiment **of the knowledge and of the truth**. St. Paul brings such a one forward, with all his boasted privileges—and prepares for a ruthless cross-examination.

21 you then who teach *the* other, do you not teach
yourself? You who herald not to steal, do you
steal?
22 You who say not to commit adultery, do you
commit adultery? You who abominate idols,
do you commit sacrilege?
23 You who boast in *the* Law, through your
transgression of the Law, do you dishonor
God?
24 For "the Name of God is blasphemed among
the nations because of you," just as it is writ-
ten.

He begins his cross-examination with a series of terse, rhetorical questions. The Jew **teaches the other**—but does he **not teach** himself? Paul focuses here on the Jew's sins, exposing his inconsistency. His following questions are very pointed in the original Greek, each question consisting of a single word of inquiry, all reaching their target like three cracks of a whip. The Jew **herald**s and preaches that men should **not steal**—but does he **steal** himself? He says that the Gentiles **should not commit adultery**—but does he **commit adultery** himself? He **abominates idols** well enough—but does he **commit sacrilege**, such as robbing the idols' temples? He is good at **boast**ing how wonderful God's Law is, honoring it with his praise—but does he turn around then and **dishonor God** who gave that Law through his **transgression** of it? Indeed he does! The proof? Even in his own Law it is proverbial that "**the Name of God is blasphemed among the nations**" because of him (Is. 52:5).

25 **For circumcision indeed profits, if you practice *the* Law, but if you are a transgressor of *the* Law, your circumcision has become uncircumcision.**
26 **If therefore the uncircumcision keep the just-requirements of the Law, will not his uncircumcision be reckoned for circumcision?**
27 **And the uncircumcision by nature, fulfilling the Law, will judge you who through the letter and circumcision *are* a transgressor of *the* Law.**
28 **For he is not a Jew who is one outwardly, neither *is* circumcision that which is outward in the flesh,**
29 **but he *is* a Jew who is one hiddenly and circumcision *is* that of *the* heart, in *the* Spirit, not in *the* letter, and *his* praise *is* not from men, but from God.**

What is the conclusion of this, and what does Jewish inconsistency mean? Does it mean that circumcision and Jewishness are of no value? They *are* of value and *do* **profit**—*if* one **practices *the* Law**. The pious Jew who practices the Law does indeed have a reward from God. But if he does not practice the Law, but thieves, commits adultery, and robs temples, and thus is **a transgressor of *the* Law**, then his **circumcision** alone cannot save him. Then it has no value at all. It is the same as if it **has become uncircumcision**.

Thus, for the Jew, *circumcision alone is of no value when it comes to being judged.* That being the case, will not **the uncircumcision**—the Gentile—if he **keep the just-requirements of the Law**, walking in honesty, chastity, and humility—will not this one be reckoned and judged as if he were circumcised? For what alone matters in the judgment is keeping the requirements of the Law. Indeed, the uncircumcised but righteous Gentile who **fulfills the Law**, on the Last

Day, **will judge** and surpass the unrighteous Jew who has the **letter** of the Law (preserved on the Torah scrolls) and **circumcision** (as a mere national badge), but who is nonetheless **a transgressor of *the* Law**.

This is because being a Jew is not meant to be merely a national reality, but also a spiritual one. It is not simply a matter of being **one outwardly**. Nor is the true significance of circumcision simply a matter of an **outward** operation **in the flesh**. Rather, a true Jew is one who is so **hiddenly**, in the inner man. It is a matter of loving God. The significance of circumcision is that it is meant to signify a tender **heart**, open and loving to God and men (see Deut. 10:16; Jer. 4:4). This inner reality is the work of the **Spirit**, not of the outward **letter** and literal surgery. A true Jew's **praise** and honor come **not from men**. That is, the Jews' international reputation for stubborn faithfulness to their God counts for nothing. What does count is whether or not God Himself thinks one faithful to Him. The approval that comes **from God** is all that really matters.

§II.3 Jews, though having the Law, still under the power of sin

The apostle then takes the next step. He has shown that sin is judged and righteousness rewarded in all men, both Jew and Gentile. But then an objection arises: if the Jews do not have immunity from God's judgment or enjoy the advantages of divine favoritism (having a special "in" with the Almighty, as it were), then what is the point of being a Jew? His unseen Jewish disputant takes it for granted that the Jews are not to be judged as other races are. Israel may be unfaithful and sinful, but God, in order to be faithful to His covenant with them, is obliged to bless them nonetheless.

St. Paul answers these objections, considering the arguments one by one. He does this by putting the Judaizers' objections in the form of questions (vv. 3, 5, 7) and then responding to them vigorously, with condensed logic.

3 1 Then what *is* the remarkable *thing* about the Jew? Or what is the profit of circumcision?
2 Much in every way! First indeed, they were entrusted with the oracles of God.
3 For what *then*? If some were unfaithful, will their unfaithfulness nullify the faithfulness of God?
4 May it never be! Rather let God be true, though every man *be found* false, just as it is written, "That You might be justified in Your words and might conquer when You are judged."
5 But if our unrighteousness commends the righteousness of God, what shall we say? *Is* the God who brings on wrath unrighteous? (I speak according to man.)
6 May it never be! Otherwise how will God judge the world?
7 But if through my falsehood the truth of God abounded to His glory, why am I also still judged as a sinner?
8 And *why* not do wicked *things* that good *things* may come? (as we are slandered and as some affirm *that* we *ourselves* say—the judgment *against them* is just!)

Paul begins by voicing the objection of his Judaizing disputant. If on the Last Day the righteous Gentile can have the same reward as the righteous Jew, what then is **the remarkable thing about** being a **Jew** at all? If **circumcision** does not ensure divine favoritism and privilege, what is the **profit** and point of it? Is there *any* advantage in belonging to the Chosen People?

Much! replies the apostle—indeed, **much in every way** one can think of! **First** and most importantly—to mention no other of the many advantages—the Jews **were entrusted with the oracles of God**, the Divine Scriptures. The phrase *the oracles of God* is a strong phrase, denoting the absolute and divine authority of the Scriptures. The religious writings of Israel, though human products, were also equally divine, containing the very words of God. And this entrusting of Israel made them no ordinary nation, for they were given a stewardship of divine revelation, with the attendant responsibility to spread it to all the world. They were not called (as they thought) to privilege alone, but also to responsibility. They were not to keep the treasure hidden for themselves, but, as a prophetic people, they were to teach the world and be a blessing to all nations.

"But," Paul's Judaizing disputant continues, "even if **some** in Israel **were unfaithful** to God [or 'untrustworthy'—the root word for *entrust* in v. 2 and for *faithful/unfaithful* in v. 3 is the same], even if they have misunderstood their call and rejected their Messiah, God still has to bless them, regardless. Otherwise **the faithfulness of God** to His covenant will be **nullified**. For God is obliged to bless His Chosen People!"

The apostle rejects such a line of thought, saying, **May it never be!**—recoiling with a strong expression of horror. Rather **God** must **be true**, even though it means that **every man** ***be found*** **false**. That is, God must do justly and judge sin, being upright and true, no matter how many in Israel are to be condemned as false. In proof of this, he quotes from Ps. 51:4, to the effect that God **will be justified in** His **words** of condemnation and will **conquer** and prevail when He is **judged**, entering into judgment with men. For He did this when He condemned even the great King David for his sin with Bathsheba and judged him through the death of David's son (2 Sam. 11—12). If God could condemn even King David for his unfaithfulness to Him, He could surely judge all.

"Yet," Paul's opponent continues, "if *that* is the case, then **our unrighteousness commends** and underscores **the righteousness of God**! The more wicked we are, the more His own glorious justice shines through when He judges us. Thus He can never **bring on wrath** to and utterly disown sinners in Israel, for that would be **unrighteous**, since their sin redounds to His glory."

This line of argument St. Paul rejects also, saying that it is

according to man, merely human reasoning. He categorically recoils, saying again, **May it never be!** For if it is indeed the case that God is **unrighteous** to **bring on wrath** to those who are unfaithful, **how will** He **judge the world** at all?—and it is agreed by all that God will one day judge the world.

"But yet," the disputant persists, "if **through my falsehood** and unfaithfulness, **the truth of God abounded to His glory**—if sinful inconstancy shows how glorious is God's faithfulness in comparison—then it is unfair that I should **still** be **judged as a sinner**! For by blessing Israel even when rebellious, God shows how merciful He truly is."

The apostle says that is as manifestly ridiculous as saying, **And *why* not do wicked *things* that good *things* may come**—for, obviously, good results cannot come from evil actions. (This, he adds in an ironic parenthesis, is how *he* is usually **slandered** and what **some affirm *that*** he himself **says**—though of course he actually says nothing of the kind. He is the one who is usually accused by the Judaizers of being soft on sin—by people whose sentence of condemnation is **just**. They are scarcely worth replying to.)

Thus, St. Paul concludes his argument with his Jewish opponents. They have argued that if Paul is correct in saying that the Jews have no immunity from judgment, then God is unjust to His covenant. The apostle refutes these arguments, showing their logical inconsistency.

He next goes on to show that, not only do the Jews *not* have an immunity from divine judgment, they are also under the power of sin just like the Gentiles—and thus in need of a Gospel to save them.

9 What then? Are we *Jews* better than they? Not
at all, for we have preaccused that both Jews
and Greeks are all under sin,
10 just as it is written, "There is not a righteous
***one*, not even one.**
11 "There is not *one* who is insightful, there is

not *one* who seeks for God;
12 "all have bowed-aside, together they have be-
come useless; there is not *one* who does kind-
ness, there is not even one.
13 "An opened grave *is* their throat, with their
tongues they *used* guile. Poison of asps *is* un-
der their lips,
14 "whose mouth is full of cursing and bitterness;
15 "swift are their feet to spill blood;
16 "ruin and misery *are* in their ways,
17 "and a way of peace they have not known.
18 "There is no fear of God before their eyes."
19 Now we know that whatever the Law says, it
speaks to those in the Law, that every mouth
may be shut up and all the world may be un-
der judgment to God,
20 because by works of *the* Law no flesh will be
justified before Him, for through *the* Law *comes*
the real-knowledge of sin.

St. Paul then comes to his point, saying, **What then? Are we *Jews* better than they** [the Gentiles]? That is, when it comes to living on a superior plane, floating above the world of sin, guilt, and judgment, do the Jews enjoy any advantage? **Not at all**, he answers, for he has **preaccused** and already charged that **both Jews and Greeks are all under** the power of **sin**.

How does he prove this? It is obvious to his Judaizing disputants that, of course, the Gentiles are **under sin** and are guilty. But not Israel! Therefore St. Paul brings forward citation after citation from the Scriptures to indict Israel of sin, drawing mostly from their well-used and beloved Psalter and from their great and popular Prophet Isaiah.

He cites Psalm 14:1–3: **"There is not a righteous *one*, not even one. There is not *one* who is insightful, there is not *one* who seeks for God; all have bowed-aside, together they have become useless; there is not *one* who does kindness, there is not even one."** That is, apostasy and sin are everywhere, with none exempt. Sin is not just the rare exception; it is the universal norm.

He cites Psalm 5:9: **"An opened grave *is* their throat, with their tongues they *used* guile."** Their speech is full of treachery, resulting in death. He cites Psalm 140:3: **"Poison of asps *is* under their lips."** Their words are stinging, painful, and lethal. He cites Psalm 10:7: **"whose mouth is full of cursing and bitterness."** All their conversation is aimed at hurting others and causing distress. He cites Isaiah 59:7, 8: **"Swift are their feet to spill blood; ruin and misery *are* in their ways, and a way of peace they have not known."** They are eager to kill and maim; they have never walked in kindness. He cites Psalm 36:1: **"There is no fear of God before their eyes."** That is, they have no piety or constraint at all in their life.

In all these last citations, reference is made to parts of the body—the throat, the tongue, the lips, the mouth, the feet, the eyes. In other words, from head to foot, from top to bottom, man is in rebellion against God, using all his bodily members as instruments of sin. *All* men are rebels and *all parts* of man are in rebellion. It is a picture of unrelieved hostility to God.

This is the picture that the Jews have of the Gentile world. Paul does not dispute this. But here he proves that it applies to Israel as well. For, he says, **we know that whatever the Law says, it speaks to those in the Law**, that is, in covenant with God. The Scriptures (including the Law, the Prophets, and the Writings) are addressed to Israel, the covenant People of God. What is the point, he asks, of God giving to Israel moral instruction and exhortation that apply only to the Gentiles? Obviously, these things are said to rebuke *Jewish* sin—not the sin of Gentiles (who would probably never read the Scriptures). And the aim is **that every mouth may be shut up and all the world**—including Israel—**may be under judgment to God** and accountable to Him.

Thus the Jews are not **better** than the Gentiles, but are **under sin** like them. Their Law does not give immunity from guilt and judgment. On the contrary, **by works of *the* Law no flesh will be justified** before God. Being physically circumcised and keeping the Sabbath—that is, being good Jews—does not give such immunity.

Such ritual badges of Jewishness (which is what St. Paul means here by *works of the Law*) cannot guarantee acceptance by God. The Judaizers, like all Jews, think that merely *having* the Law, merely hearing it read in synagogue on the Sabbath as a good Jew, somehow will justify them (see 2:13). St. Paul denies this is the case. That, he says, is not the function of the Law. Indeed, so far from ensuring exemption from judgment on sin, the Law actually brings sin into clearer focus and reality, for **through *the* Law *comes* the real-knowledge of sin**. (Note: not just knowledge—Gr. *gnosis*, but *real*-knowledge and intimate acquaintance—Gr. *epignosis.*) For (as the apostle will later detail in 7:1f), the Law is powerless to overcome addictive sin in a person's life. Its task is to define and forbid sin, not to eradicate it.

§II.4 All are now justified by faith—as was Abraham

St. Paul has shown how Jew and Gentile are alike. Both are under sin, and Jewish circumcision and other works of the Law are no help to the Jew in avoiding the divine judgment on this sin. And as both are alike in their plight, so both are offered the same rescue—the righteousness of God, His forgiveness and benevolence (see 1:17). This same remedy of the Gospel preached by Paul is the universal remedy offered for the healing of all men everywhere, both Jew and Gentile. Paul's Judaizing detractors are wrong in saying that circumcision is necessary and that men must thus become Jews in order to know full salvation. Salvation is by faith alone, not by faith plus circumcision. The Gentile who emerged from the waters of baptism to walk in newness of life (see 6:4) does not need to be circumcised to be justified and forgiven by God. The obedience of faith is enough.

21 But now without *the* Law *the* righteousness of
God has been manifested, being witnessed to
by the Law and the Prophets—
22 the righteousness of God through faith in Jesus

Christ for all those who have faith, for there is
no distinction
23 (for all have sinned and lack the glory of God),
24 being justified *as a* gift by His grace through
the redemption which *is* in Christ Jesus,
25 whom God put forward *as a* propitiation,
through faith, by His Blood, for a demonstra-
tion of His righteousness, in respect of the pass-
ing over the preoccurring sins
26 in the forbearance of God for the demonstra-
tion of His righteousness at the present time,
that He might be Himself just and justify the
one who *has* faith in Jesus.

The apostle comes to his point, for which he has been preparing since 1:18. **Now**, since the coming of Christ, **without *the* Law** and completely apart from any obligation to fulfill Jewish ritual requirements, the **righteousness of God** has been **manifested** through the Gospel. That is what Jesus and His ministry, death, and Resurrection were all about—manifesting the righteousness of God and His free forgiveness and bestowal of new life. This salvation and Kingdom were **witnessed to by the Law and the Prophets**. All the Jewish Scriptures foretold it. Now it has come.

This righteousness and divine benevolence are experienced **through faith in Jesus Christ**. If one will but accept the apostolic Gospel and be baptized, living as a disciple of Jesus, one can experience God's kindness and salvation. It is thus available **to all those who have faith**, without any **distinction** between Jew and Gentile. (This is only fitting, St. Paul adds parenthetically, for **all have sinned**—Jews and Gentiles alike—and all **lack the glory of God**. All have equally gone astray like lost sheep, living as fallen men in a fallen world, destitute of the divine glory with which Adam was clothed in the Garden. There is no distinction between Jew and Gentile in their fallenness; there should be no distinction between them in their way to salvation.) Both are **justified *as a* gift** (Gr. *dorean*, "gratuitously, for nothing") **by His grace**. That is, both are

EXCURSUS:

On Propitiation and the Love of God

The concept of propitiation and expiation was one familiar to all the ancients and was assumed to be so by the apostle as he wrote to his first-century audience. It is unfamiliar, however, to us moderns and rings unnaturally in our ears. When we hear of propitiating God or placating His wrath, we too easily construct an unworthy picture of God in our minds, anthropomorphically remaking Him in our image and imagining Him to be irritable and cranky like us, needing to be calmed down. We form a picture of an irate Deity, one needing sacrifices to placate Him. Obviously this is not who God is, and the scriptural concept of propitiating the divine wrath should not be understood in this way.

In coming to terms with concepts of expiation, several things need to be kept in mind.

Firstly, man in his rebellious mind is hateful to God. We see this in situations where we clearly acknowledge the hideousness of the rebellion. In the case of the Nazi brutalities, for example, we have no trouble acknowledging that such things must be hateful to God if God is good. A holy and good God could only regard such things with loathing. The ancients knew that *all* prideful rebellion was hateful to heaven. Sometimes we cannot see our own sins and imagine that God must be a bit oversensitive if He hates them. But it is not that God is oversensitive; it is that we are blind.

Secondly, such willful rebellion puts the moral fabric of the universe out of kilter. Our acts *really matter*. God's holiness and justice are the foundation upon which the universe is built (see Ps. 10:3; 89:14). If the harmony of the moral order is shattered by our sin, this cannot just be ignored. The blood of the innocent cries to heaven for justice; blood shed by the wicked and not avenged pollutes the land

(Gen. 4:10; Num. 35:33). When such sin is committed, God in His holiness and justice cannot simply pretend it never happened. It must be dealt with. The sinner does not need only to be forgiven. He needs to be *cleansed*. His sin cannot simply be passed over. It needs to be *expiated*.

Thirdly, this expiation is by sacrifice. That is, sin introduces death into the life of the universe. This death needs to be replaced and supplanted by life. Sacrifice is essentially the offering of life—taking the thing sacrificed and using its life to make good a spiritual imbalance in the fabric of the world. In the thought of the ancients, the life of anything is contained in its blood (Lev. 17:11), so that without the shedding of blood in sacrifice, there can be no forgiveness of sin (see Heb. 9:22).

It follows then that the demand for propitiation by God does not mean that God is not loving or that He is somehow irritable or vengeful. Rather, it means that sin is a reality and can only be removed by other realities. Sin always brings disruption and death; it can only be healed by the offering of life. God's love is proven in that He Himself provides the means of propitiation and of new life—even the Blood of Christ.

forgiven freely, as baptized disciples of Christ, by God's unmerited favor. God has not put them on parole, awaiting the satisfaction of further ritual requirements in order to forgive them. Their forgiveness is fully bestowed at baptism.

Thus, justification and forgiveness do not depend upon circumcision. Their root and source is not human effort and the drive toward self-vindication. Their source is **the redemption which *is* in Christ Jesus.** The word translated *redemption* is the Greek word *apolutrosis,* the root word of which is *lutrosis,* meaning "to buy back." The word was often used in antiquity to refer to the buying back of slaves from captivity. St. Paul means here that we are all slaves of sin, fettered by mortality, in bondage to the enemy, but Christ has set us free, buying us back to be the slaves and sons of God. Our forgiveness is rooted in this liberation.

How is this accomplished? By the Cross of Christ. His death was no mere execution or martyrdom. It was a sacrifice, which God **put forward** or planned (see the use of this verb in 1:13) in His eternal design to save the world. Christ's **Blood** and death was, by God's design, to be a **propitiation**, its benefit received **through faith** (without any supplementary circumcision). The word translated *propitiation* is the Greek *ilasterion,* which means "that which expiates sin and placates God, making Him merciful [Gr. *ileos*]." It is the word used in the Greek of Exodus 25:16 for the "mercy seat" or lid of the Ark of the Covenant, where the sacrificial blood was sprinkled on the Day of Atonement (Lev. 16:14), bringing cleansing to Israel so that the Holy God could continue dwelling in their midst. The word is used also in 4 Maccabees 17:22 to describe the martyrdom of the righteous under Antiochus Epiphanes, saying that it was through these deaths that Israel was purified of sin. By using this word, St. Paul means that Christ's death on the Cross was the expiatory sacrifice by which the sins of the world were taken away and the world reconciled to God. All people in antiquity understood the concept of propitiation and how sacrifices could avert the divine wrath and make atonement (see Num. 16:46–48). The apostle says that Christ's death was just such an atonement.

This demonstrates God's **righteousness** and compassion to men, because He thus **passes over** all of the world's **preoccurring sins**, forgiving them and not taking them into account, treating them as if they had never existed. This shows His great **forbearance** and patience **at the present time** of the Gospel. Through the sacrifice of Christ, God is willing to forgive whatever went before, withholding His judgment.

Thus, He is not only **just** and good (Gr. *dikaios*—an attribute often linked with mercy, e.g. Ps. 116:5 LXX). He is also the One who **justifies** anyone who has **faith in Jesus**, forgiving him freely, regardless of his race. As St. John Chrysostom says, commenting upon this passage, "Not only is He Himself living, He also makes the dead to live." The Cross thus shows the boundless depth of

God's compassion. He is just and merciful in **Himself** and He shows this by **justifying** (Gr. *dikaioo*) all who approach Him.

27 **Where therefore *is* the boasting? It is excluded. By what kind of law? Of works? No, but through a law of faith.**
28 **For we reckon that a man is justified by faith, without works of *the* Law.**
29 **Or *is He* God of Jews only? Is He not the God of Gentiles also? Yes, of Gentiles also,**
30 **if indeed God *is* one, and He will justify *the* circumcision by faith and the uncircumcision through the faith.**
31 **Do we therefore nullify *the* Law through faith? May it never be! But we make *the* Law to stand!**

So, St. Paul continues, **Where therefore *is* the boasting** of the Jew? It is **excluded**—not by a **law** or principle **of works**, but by the principle **of faith**. That is, the Jew has no reason to boast of his Jewishness *not* because he is no longer Jewish. Rather, he cannot boast because these works are no longer relevant to his forgiveness. He is **justified** and forgiven **by faith, without works of *the* Law**. His circumcision contributes nothing. God looks only to any man's faith and commitment to Him.

This, of course, is in a way consistent with what Judaism has said all along. For Yahweh is not the God **of Jews only**, but the one true God of all the earth and **of Gentiles also**—since, as Israel confesses, **God *is* One** (Deut. 6:4) and there are no other gods but Him. Obviously then, He is the **God of Gentiles** as well as of the Jews, and it is fitting that He should relate to both equally. Faith is the means whereby both are saved—the Jew being saved **by faith** (Gr. *ek pisteos*) and the Gentile **through the faith** (Gr. *dia tes pisteos*). The difference in the prepositions used here may be simply stylistic. But it seems more likely that the apostle is referring to a subtle nuance. The Jew, though having the Law, is nonetheless saved *by faith*, not by keeping the Law and being Jewish. The Gentile, not having the Law, is saved *through that faith* alone. There remains thus a difference between the two. But they have this in common: what saves them both is their faith.

Does the fact that the Law of Moses contributes nothing to being forgiven mean that the **Law** is **nullified through faith**? Does it mean that faith in Christ somehow invalidates the Law and shows it to be worthless? **May it never be!** the apostle cries out, horrified at the thought. On the contrary, he insists, we Christians **make *the* Law to stand**. That is, we do not live lawlessly, rejecting the good things the Law inculcates. Rather, set free from sin by our faith in Christ, we *keep* the Law, fulfilling it by our life of love (see 13:10), thus establishing the Law as valid in our lives. Walking by faith does not mean walking immorally, not caring for what God wants (as the Judaizing detractors allege). Rather, it means to fulfill the precepts of the Law all the more zealously.

4 1 **What therefore shall we say that Abraham, our father according to the flesh, has found?**

2 **For if Abraham was justified by works, he has *grounds for* boasting (but not before God).**

3 **For what does the Scripture say? "Abraham had faith in God and it was reckoned to him for righteousness."**

4 **Now to the one who works, the reward is not reckoned according to grace, but according to debt.**

5 **But to the one who does not work, but has faith in Him who justifies the impious, his faith is reckoned for righteousness.**

Then St. Paul deals with an objection of his Judaizing opponent. "If God justifies all—both Jew and Gentile—without works of the Jewish Law," the Jew asks, "then what is the significance of Abraham, **our father according to the flesh**? For Abraham is the father of the faithful, and he was given the covenant of circumcision. How then can one be his spiritual descendant without sharing that circumcision?"

The apostle sets out to answer this question, and in so doing puts the Jewish Law within the wider context of God's prior promise to Abraham.

First, he acknowledges that **if Abraham was** indeed **justified by works**, then he **has grounds for boasting**. That is, if he was forgiven his sins and made the Friend of God because he was circumcised, then he was indeed better than other men who were not circumcised. But (Paul hastily adds, in a parenthesis) that still does not give him grounds to boast **before God**! In other words, he is still not immune from the divine judgment—for the Jews seem to think that being circumcised means that they will not be judged as other men are.

But, St. Paul asks, was Abraham in fact justified by works and forgiven because he was circumcised? **What does the Scripture** actually **say**? Well, Paul says, quoting Genesis 15:6, it says that **Abraham had faith** (Gr. *episteusen*) **in God and it was reckoned to him for righteousness**. That is, it says that he was justified *by faith* (Gr. *pistis*) and not by works. The proof? That his righteousness and vindication was **reckoned to him**. For, St. Paul reasons, if something is reckoned or credited to someone, it is obviously a matter of **grace** (Gr. *charis*) and not of **debt** (Gr. *opheilema*)—of being given a favor, not of being given what is due. For no one who has earned his wage speaks of that wage being credited or reckoned to him, but simply of receiving what is owed. That Abraham's righteousness was reckoned to him indicates that he received it not as a matter of obligation on God's part, but as an act of grace. Abraham did not deserve this righteousness and his standing before God, but it was reckoned to him anyway. Thus, **the one who works** receives his **reward** as a matter of debt; **the one who does not work**, but instead **has faith** and trusts the One **who justifies** even **the impious**, receives it as a matter of that **faith** being **reckoned** and credited to him **for righteousness**.

In all this discussion, the apostle is appealing to the original experience of Abraham. The Patriarch at that time had no child or heir. Nonetheless, God promised him that his reward would be very great and that he would be given a child as heir, and, through that child, he would have as many descendants as the stars in the sky. Despite the advanced age of both himself and his wife, Abraham had faith in God and believed His promise, and it was on the basis of that faith that righteousness was reckoned to him and he became the Friend of God, inheriting His covenant.

This phrase, *it was reckoned to him for righteousness,* was used elsewhere in the Old Testament. In Ps. 106:31, it was used to describe the zealous act of Phineas, who slew an apostate idolater who had brought a plague of judgment upon Israel (Num. 25:1–13). For this, Phineas was given "a covenant of perpetual priesthood" (Num. 25:13), so that his descendants should be priests throughout the generations. The Psalmist describes this by saying that his act was "reckoned to him for righteousness." That is, the immensity of the reward was out of all proportion to the deed done. For because of one single act of zeal, his descendants throughout all generations were blessed. Phineas was not owed such a great reward, but it was bestowed on him anyway. It was the same with Abraham. Because of a single act of faith and steadfast trust in God, he was rewarded with numberless descendants, so as to be a father of many nations (see Gen. 17:5). This was clearly not a case of his earning such a recompense. In the words of St. Paul, it was not **according to debt** or what he was owed by God. It was a matter of undeserved reward, **according to grace**. St. Paul's point in all this is to show how this unearned reward was reckoned to Abraham because he *had faith in God*—and not because of anything he had done (such as circumcision).

6 Even as David also speaks of the blessing of the man to whom God reckons righteousness without works:

7 "**Blessed are *those* whose lawless *acts* have been forgiven, and whose sins have been covered-over.**
8 "**Blessed *is* the man to whom *the* Lord will not reckon sin.**"

And not just Abraham, but David too. St. Paul cites both the founder of the Jewish nation—Abraham—and also its great exemplar of holiness—David, the man after God's own heart and the author of Israel's sublime Psalter. **David also speaks of the blessing of the man to whom God reckons righteousness without works.** That is, it is not just the experience of Abraham that proves that God will vindicate and accept a man apart from his earning it. The experience of David proves the same. How? Because David wrote in Psalm 32:1, 2, "**Blessed are *those* whose lawless *acts* have been forgiven, and whose sins have been covered-over. Blessed *is* the man to whom *the* Lord will not reckon sin.**" That is, even the sinful man, the one who has committed **lawless *acts*** (Gr. *anomiai*) and who does not keep the Law (Gr. *Nomos*)—even this one can know the blessing of God. For God forgives him and vindicates him, not because he has earned it (obviously he hasn't), but because he trusts in God and turns to Him in penitence. Thus, St. Paul argues, keeping the precepts of the Law (such as circumcision) *cannot* be the basis on which God accepts a man. For God will bless even the penitent sinner who has *not* kept the Law.

9 **Is this blessing then upon the circumcision, or upon the uncircumcision also? For we say, "Faith was reckoned to Abraham for righteousness."**
10 **How then was it reckoned? Being in circumcision or in uncircumcision? Not in circumcision, but in uncircumcision.**
11 **And he received a sign of circumcision, a seal**

of the righteousness of the faith which *he had*
in the uncircumcision, that he might be father
of all who have faith *while* in uncircumcision,
that righteousness might be reckoned to them,
12 and father of circumcision to those not of the
circumcision only, but also to those who walk-
straight in the steps of the faith of our father
Abraham, which he had *while* in uncircumcision.

So a **blessing** is given to those who trust God, as David did. But does one have to be circumcised in order to receive it? Paul's Judaizing adversaries do not dispute that God justifies and forgives the penitent and that He blesses those who come to Him. But they assert that this blessing is **upon the circumcision** only, and that it is for Jews alone, not for the Gentile **uncircumcision**. It is this blessing that Abraham received and to which the Scriptures refer, saying, "**Faith was reckoned to Abraham for righteousness.**" Like David, Abraham also received a mighty blessing beyond his deserving. The question then is: Does one have to be a Jew in order to be justified?

St. Paul returns to the personal history of Abraham for the answer. It was clear from the Genesis narratives that Abraham was in fact reckoned righteous and made the Friend of God and inheritor of His promise, **not in circumcision, but in uncircumcision**. That is, he was not yet circumcised when God promised him that he would indeed have a son, and when he believed that promise he was reckoned by God to be righteous (Gen. 15:1–6). By legalistic Jewish standards, he was then not yet a Jew, but still a Gentile! It was only later that he was circumcised (Gen. 17:9–24). Thus, it is apparent that the divine blessing cannot be conditional upon the fulfillment of a legalistic and ritual requirement such as circumcision, for that blessing was given to Abraham *before* he fulfilled the requirement. The only unconditional requirement to be fulfilled was faith.

What then is the relationship of circumcision to faith, and of ritual works to justification? That of sign and seal. That is, the significance of circumcision (as of any of the works of the Jewish Law) is that it embodies and points to the inner realities of the heart.

What God wanted from Abraham was faith—an abiding trust in His love and willingness to follow Him regardless of the cost. It was by fulfilling this divine demand that Abraham was reckoned righteous and received an unearned blessing. The circumcision which he later received was a **sign** of this. It was its **seal**, certifying and proving the genuineness of the blessing he received.

Thus, Abraham is truly a universal father, the archetype of faith for all the world. That is what is meant by his being "the father of a multitude of nations" (Gen. 17:5). He does not belong only to the Jewish nation, but to all the world—to all who will **have faith** and trust in the One God. The **righteousness of faith** was reckoned to him while he was uncircumcised precisely to show that he belongs to all the world, and not to the Jews alone.

Thus, faith is what matters, and faith is what constitutes one as Abraham's true descendant. The Gentiles or nations (the same word, *ethne,* is used for both English words)—those who have **faith *while* in uncircumcision**—are his true descendants, equally with the Jews. For the Jews are of course also his true descendants—provided they not only are **of the circumcision**, but also **walk-straight in the steps of the faith of our father Abraham which he had *while* in uncircumcision**. The verb here translated *walk-straight* is the Greek *stoicheo*, which means literally "to walk in a straight line" (from *stoichos*, "row"). The thought is of walking in precisely the same path as the one ahead, of following faithfully without deviation. Merely to be circumcised is not enough to qualify one as Abraham's true descendant. One must also imitate Abraham's faith, trusting in God as he did, not deviating from the course of faith by walking into the dead-end of Jewish legalism.

13 **For not through *the* Law was the promise to Abraham or to his seed that he would be heir of the world, but through *the* righteousness of faith.**

14 **For if those *who are* of the Law *are* heirs, faith**

is made empty and the promise *is* nullified;
15 for the Law works out wrath (but where there
is no law, neither *is there* transgression).
16 Therefore, *it is* by faith, according to grace, that
the promise may be confirmed to all the seed,
not to those who are of the Law only, but also
to those of *the* faith of Abraham, who is father
of us all
17 (as it is written, "A father of many nations
have I set you"), in the sight of Him whom
he had faith in, *even* God, who *is* life-giving
to the dead and calls into existence what did
not exist.

The apostle continues to reflect on the relationship of Abraham with the Jewish nation. For Paul's Jewish opponents look to Abraham not so much as the forerunner and embodiment of **faith**, but as the forerunner of the **Law**. For them, the fact that Abraham received the covenant of circumcision (which rite was later a part of the Mosaic Law) means that Abraham and his covenantal blessing belong as exclusively to Israel as does the Law. The Gentile nations have no share in the Mosaic Law, and they have no share in Israel's "father according to the flesh" (v. 1) either.

St. Paul vehemently denies this. Abraham is the embodiment of faith, and he is thus the father of all who share that faith, be they Jew or Gentile. For **the promise to Abraham or to his seed that he would be heir of the world**—the covenant God made with him, in which he was declared righteous and the Friend of God—was **not through *the* Law**, but was **through *the* righteousness of faith**. The apostle is emphatic that God's purpose in calling Abraham is a cosmic one, embracing all the world.

Abraham was not to be merely the first name on someone's family tree, the progenitor of a single nation (as Esau, for example, was the progenitor of the nation of Edom). Rather, he is a spiritual figure, the paradigm and embodiment of faith, accessible to all. That is the purpose and spirit of the promise made to him. When God said,

"You shall be the father of a multitude of nations" (Gen. 17:5), and promised that Abraham's descendants would be as numberless as the stars (Gen. 22:17), He meant not merely that Isaac, Ishmael, Jacob, and Esau were to have many descendants. The thought here is spiritual and cosmic, not narrowly national. God meant that *all* earth's families were to be blessed in Abraham (Gen. 12:3) and that *all* nations were to look to him as their father. That is why St. Paul characterizes God's promise to Abraham as saying that he **would be heir of the world**—not just heir of Palestine. For if his descendants were only the Jewish nation, then one could say indeed that he would, through his descendants, be heir to the Promised Land. But in fact his descendants were meant to include *all* nations of the world—and thus he is heir to all the world, not just Palestine. Abraham was called by God to belong to us all.

When this is comprehended, it is apparent that this **promise** and calling cannot be realized through so narrow and national an instrument as the Law of Moses. If one has to be Jewish, circumcised, and an adherent **of the Law** to inherit the promise made to Abraham's seed, then obviously that **promise is nullified** and the **faith** in God on which it is focused is **made empty**. For God's promise to Abraham was that he would be father to many nations/Gentiles (Gr. *ethne*). If that means (as the logic of the Judaizers insinuates) that these nations must all become Jewish in order to be so blessed, then that promise is useless—for the Gentiles cannot become Jewish and still remain Gentile. The promise to Abraham holds out universal faith in the One God as its goal and content. If Jews only can inherit such a promise, then the universality of that faith is indeed emptied of all content—for a universal faith held only by a few is a contradiction in terms.

In fact, the Law of Moses is incapable of being the instrument for fulfilling God's promise to Abraham. For the Law is by nature conditional: it produces blessings if one obeys and **wrath** if one disobeys (see Deut. 28). (St. Paul adds in a parenthesis that **where there is no law, neither *is there* transgression**. That is, when one walks in the realm of faith, transcending the Law, one is then also free from transgression and guilt. As Paul later writes, "Sin shall not be lord over us, for we are not under the Law but under grace" [6:14]. He writes this here to show how the Law is not necessary to avoid transgression.)

If one depends on the Law as the instrument for realizing the covenantal blessing of Abraham, then all God's work is left in question. Not only would the Jews alone realize what was meant to be for all the nations, but not even all of them would realize and possess the blessing. For the history of Israel is largely the history of disobedience and wrath—as their historical Scriptures abundantly testify. If God's universal covenant with the world needs the Law of Moses to bring it into effect, then that covenant is doomed to be almost completely ineffectual. The Mosaic Law does indeed have a purpose—but realizing the universal covenant of Abraham is not it!

For God's purpose in calling Abraham is to be **confirmed** and sure **to all the seed** and to *all* his descendants—not only to his Jewish descendants, **who are of the Law**, but **also to those** Gentiles who are **of *the* faith of Abraham**. That is why he is called **father of us all**, Gentiles as well as Jews. And that is why the promise to Abraham is not realized by the Mosaic Law, but rather **by faith, according to grace**. The Abrahamic blessing is given to anyone of any nation who will share his faith and receive God's blessing given freely, by grace, apart from any deserving. That was the real reason it was **written** that he was **set** and established as **a father of many nations** (Gen. 17:5). If salvation is by faith (and not by Jewish works of Law), then all the world can be assured of sharing the blessing of Abraham.

This Abraham is described as standing **in the sight of Him whom he had faith in, *even* God**, as a kind of witness to the efficacy of faith. The word translated here *in the sight of* (Gr. *katenanti*) means "opposite, before." It is used in Luke 19:30, where the disciples are instructed to go into the village "opposite" them. Its use here is meant to bring to mind a picture of Abraham walking before God in faith (see Gen. 17:1), and by that faith abiding under God's watchful care.

The effectual power of that care in which Abraham trusted

is described as that which is **life-giving to the dead** and able to **call into existence what did not exist**. That is, Abraham's faith was in the God who is able to bring the dead to life and call into being what before had no existence. It was, in fact, a faith in the resurrection.

By characterizing Abraham's faith as a faith in God's power to bring life out of death, St. Paul makes a further identification of his ancient faith with the faith of contemporary Christians. The saving faith of Abraham and the faith of Christians are one and the same, though separated by centuries, and the Christians are thus the true seed of Abraham!

18 In hope beyond hope he had faith that he might become a father of many nations, according to that which had been spoken, "Thus shall your seed be."
19 And without being weak in faith, he considered his own body, already *become* dead, being about a hundred years old, and the deadness of Sarah's womb;
20 yet, *with respect* to the promise of God, he did not discern in faithlessness, but was empowered in the faith, giving glory to God,
21 and being fully-assured that what He had promised, He had power also to do.
22 Therefore also "it was reckoned to him for righteousness."
23 Now not for him only was it written that "it was reckoned to him,"
24 but for us also, to whom it is about to be reckoned, to those who have faith on Him who raised Jesus our Lord from *the* dead,
25 who was delivered for our offenses and was raised for our justification.

St. Paul continues by showing how Abraham's faith was indeed faith in God's power to bring the dead to life. The patriarch believed God **in hope beyond hope**, believing things that were physically impossible (such as the resurrection of the dead). For God had promised him, **Thus shall your seed be**—as numberless as the stars, as the sand by the seashore (Gen. 22:17). Thus he would be **father of many nations** (Gen. 17:5). But this was impossible, for he had no physical heir and both he and his wife Sarah were as good as dead. He was living securely in a state of death (so far as having children was concerned), for he was **about a hundred years old**. His wife also was too old, well past the years for childbearing, her **womb** dead for that purpose as well. He **considered** and contemplated all this, fully taking it in.

But he was not **weak in faith**. He did not **discern in faithlessness**. The word here translated *discern* is the Greek *diakrino* (used also in 1 Cor. 14:29) and here conjures up a picture of a man debating with himself, disputing, arguing, wavering. The great Patriarch did none of that. Rather, he **was empowered in the faith, giving glory to God**. He was **fully-assured** that what God had promised, **He had power also to do**. The creeping mortality working in Abraham and Sarah's old age was no barrier to Him. Death itself must give way before His power and promise. It was because Abraham had such faith in the power of God even over death that **it was reckoned to him for righteousness**.

And that, continues St. Paul, is the same for us. Indeed, Abraham is a type of the Church, for his experience foreshadows that of the Christian. His experience of being justified by faith **when it was reckoned to him** was not **written** in the Scriptures **for him only**. Rather, it was written down **for us also** who believe in Christ. The Jews may think that Abraham's history was recorded so that they might take pride in their national heritage. Indeed, many Jews of that day did indeed rely upon what they deemed the merits of Abraham, thinking that it made up for their own deficiencies. This is entirely erroneous, according to St. Paul. Abraham does not belong to those who have none of his faith or to those who reject the

Lord Jesus (see John 8:39–44). He belongs to the Christians, to those whose faith is the same as his.

That is why the experience and history of Abraham was written in the Scriptures—to confirm and prove the faith of the Christians. As Abraham was reckoned righteous and vindicated, so the Christians also are **about to be reckoned** righteous and vindicated (the verb form indicates the certainty of the result). They will share his justification, for they also now share his faith in the God who brings life out of death, since they **have faith on Him who raised Jesus our Lord from *the* dead.** Bringing his discussion on the significance of Abraham to its conclusion, St. Paul ends with Jesus as the focus of faith. Saving Christian faith is not faith in the abstract. It is faith in Jesus Christ. We do not believe in God's power over death in the abstract, but as manifested historically in the Cross and Resurrection of Christ. It is He who brings the faith of Abraham to the Gentile nations of the earth and so fulfills God's covenant to Abraham. It was He who was **delivered for our offenses and was raised for our justification.**

We may note in passing how the Cross and Resurrection are united as the one cause and source of our salvation. It was because of our offenses and our need for justification and the forgiveness of those offenses that Christ was both delivered to the Cross and raised from the dead. This reveals that our salvation consists not simply in being forgiven or having our legal debt paid. It consists also in our triumph over death. It was through both the Cross and the Resurrection that Christ "trampled down death by death" and bestowed upon us the gift of life. It is too limited a view to suggest (as some have done) that our need consisted solely of guilt and debt and that the Cross by itself paid this debt (in a kind of substitutionary switch) so that the Resurrection was nothing more than a happy ending, contributing nothing to our justification. We were not only guilty, but dead, needing not only forgiveness, but also life and transformation. This need was met by both the Cross and the Resurrection, as the one indivisible source of our saving theosis.

§II.5 Since justified by faith, we have new life as a gift

5 1 **Having been justified therefore by faith, let us have peace with God through our Lord Jesus Christ,**
2 **through whom also we have access by faith into this grace in which we stand, and let us boast in hope of the glory of God.**

St. Paul continues his exhortation and explanation of his Gospel, arguing over the heads (one may say) of his Judaizing opponents. For they assert that mere faith is not enough. To have peace with God and enjoy His glory on the Last Day, they say, one must be circumcised as well. Having argued that one is justified by faith apart from such works of the Law, the apostle here presses his point home, urging his hearers to enter into what God has provided, telling them not to be persuaded by those who say that one also needs to be circumcised in order to enjoy peace with God.

That is why St. Paul uses the hortatory **let us have peace** rather than the indicative "we have peace." Though the two possible readings differ only in a single letter ("let us have peace" being *exomen* with an omega and "we have peace" being *exomen* with an omicron), the hortatory is by far the better-attested reading. Many versions nonetheless read it as an indicative ("we have peace"), such as the KJV, the RSV, the NASB, the TEV, the NIV, and the Catholic NAB (though the possibility of the hortatory is provided as a marginal reading), since it seems to them perhaps that the indicative suits the context better than the hortatory. That would make sense if St. Paul were writing a kind of textbook of theology and if his purpose were to outline the fruits of justification (as one commentator said).

But in fact St. Paul is not writing a textbook, but arguing a case. His Judaizing opponent has still not left the room (as it were)—as is apparent from the Jewish objection in 6:1. Paul is urging his hearers not to be persuaded by their Jewish arguments for circumcision, but to **have peace with God through our Lord Jesus Christ**—and not through circumcision. Christ alone is sufficient for us. It is through Him—without the necessity for further works such as circumcision—that we now **have access by faith** into that grace in which we stand (see Eph. 2:18). Formerly we were estranged from God by our sins, alienated from Him, like all the world. Now, through the Cross, peace has been made between God and men (Col. 2:20), and in our eucharistic worship, we can boldly approach the divine Throne and dare to address the heavenly God as "Father."

It is our discipleship to Jesus alone that gains us the boldness to approach God as His children and to experience His forgiveness and transforming power in worship. That **grace in which we stand** and enjoy the security of the divine favor comes from our commitment to Jesus alone. Through Him we can **boast in hope of the glory of God**. That is, our hope and certainty of enjoying the transfiguring Presence and glory of God (which we will put on like a garment and shine like the sun; see Matt. 13:43) is through Christ alone. Let us boast of receiving this inheritance through Him, and not rely upon the Law!

3 **And not only *that*, but let us also boast in our tribulations, knowing that the tribulation works out perseverance,**
4 **and the perseverance, provenness, and the provenness, hope,**
5 **and the hope does not put to shame, because the love of God has been poured out in our hearts through the Holy Spirit who was given to us.**

And that is not all! St. Paul urges us also to **boast** in our **tribulations** and persecutions for the sake of Christ, for those afflictions will lead us closer to that same hope! Unlike the Judaizers, with their more restricted view of the love of God, the apostle knows that God's love is overwhelming and freely poured out upon all men. That love is all that is needed to reach the glory of God. And **not only *that***, that love is so overwhelming that it can transform even our sufferings to work for our good (see 8:28). Therefore we are urged to **boast** and welcome even our **tribulations** as contributing to our glorification.

For our **tribulation works out perseverance**. That is, the more we suffer for Christ, the more we learn the severe lessons of endurance and the more spiritually hardy we become. As with athletes enduring the rigors of training, our persecution for the Lord makes us strong and able to endure. That **perseverance** in turn results in **provenness** (Gr. *dokimen*, cognate with *dokimazo*, "to prove or test"). The more we endure, the more we prove our worth, as those who have come through the fire and passed the test. (Compare the opposite term *adokimos*, "worthless," used in 1:28.) And the more proven we are, the more we have reason to be filled with **hope**—even that hope of the glory of God. And that **hope** will **not put** us **to shame** and disappoint us. Rather, what we hope for we will certainly obtain. How can we know this? **Because the love of God has been poured out in our hearts through the Holy Spirit who was given to us** in baptism. Our liturgical experience of baptism thus forms the basis for our trust in God's goodness. When we were baptized, God poured out His love into our hearts.

The verb translated here *to pour out* (Gr. *ekxeo*) means "to gush forth abundantly, to spill around." It is used in Acts 1:18 for the spilling out of Judas' bowels and in John 2:15 for the scattering of the coins of the moneychangers in the Temple. Its use here shows how abundantly God lavishes His love upon us: here is no careful portioning out of His compassion, but a reckless, drenching, unstinting shower. When the Holy Spirit is so powerfully bestowed in baptismal initiation (in what today is called chrismation), it is a testimony to the boundless love God has for believers and to our security in Him. How amazing is this love! For it causes even our sufferings to work for good.

6 For while we were still weak, at the *appointed* time, Christ died for *the* impious.

7 For one will with difficulty die for a righteous *man*, though perhaps for the good *one* someone would dare to die.

8 But God commends His own love toward us, in that while we were still sinners, Christ died for us.

9 Much more therefore, having been justified now in His Blood, we will be saved through Him from the wrath.

10 For if while we were enemies, we were reconciled to God through the death of His Son, much more, having been reconciled, we will be saved by His life.

11 And not only *that*, but also we boast in God through our Lord Jesus Christ, through whom we have now received the reconciliation.

The apostle continues to elaborate on this boundless divine love, for it shows how senseless is the objection of the Judaizers that one needs to be circumcised in order to be saved. For can anyone really suppose that this kind of loving God would wrathfully reject one who comes to Him in loving trust, simply because he has omitted a religious ritual?

For see the greatness of that love! **While we were still weak** and helpless to save ourselves, **at the *appointed* time, Christ died for *the* impious**. The ends of the ages had come (see 1 Cor. 10:11), the evening of the world. Man was sick and dying, utterly unable to restore himself to health or avoid the just sentence of divine judgment. When all seemed to be lost, Christ came, strong to save, our Healer and Restorer. He died on the Cross for us, impious and rebellious as we were, and brought us back to God.

St. Paul draws out the full significance of that death and how it reveals the immensity of God's love. In this world, he points out, **one will with difficulty die for a righteous *man***, though he admits that **perhaps** for such a **good *one* someone would dare to die.** Such goodness and moral heroism are rare, though possible. But **God commends His own love toward us, in that while we were still sinners, Christ died for us.** We were all far from being good. We **were still sinners**—those who consistently spurn God's advances and live in ways that He hates. Yet even so, Christ died for us. If dying to save a good and righteous man marks the limit of human goodness and moral heroism, then God's goodness is completely off the scale and surpasses anything in our experience. It is this love that He pours into our hearts.

Yet there is more to be expected from this love. For **if while we were enemies, we were reconciled to God through the death of His Son, much more having been reconciled we will be saved by His life.** Christ died for us while we were yet impious and rebellious against God's love. Now that we are no longer impious, but rather godly—now that we are no longer rebellious, but rather submissive to Him—how **much more** can we expect to be **saved through Him from the wrath** of God directed against the rebellious on the Last Day? Now that we, His former foes, have been **justified in His Blood** and **death**, we can expect even more to be saved by His life.

The reference to **His life** is, of course, not to His life in the flesh during His earthly ministry. Rather, it refers to His life now at the right hand of God, where He "always lives to intercede for us" (Heb. 7:25). It is, in fact, a reference to the life we receive from Him at the eucharistic chalice. For in our walk as His submissive disciples, as we strive to please Him, we can confidently expect mercy, forgiveness, and the infusion of eternal life. Such mercy was offered to us when we were His unreconciled enemies; how much more shall we have it now that we are His reconciled friends? If His death availed for us, how much more will His life? Having been raised (Rom. 4:25) and glorified to the Father's right hand, He shares that life with us as we worship Him in the Divine Liturgy He Himself established. There we receive (as St. Ignatius of Antioch said in his

Epistle to the Ephesians) "the medicine of immortality, the antidote that we should not die but live forever." As those who receive from His life-giving chalice now, we may confidently expect to be given life at His final judgment and to be **saved from the wrath**.

And there is yet more. For **not only *that***—not only do believers look to be saved from the wrath on the Last Day through their faith, not only do they boast of the future "hope of the glory of God" (v. 2)—they also **boast in God** and in what He has done for them **through our Lord Jesus Christ** *now*, in this age. Their **reconciliation** and standing with God is not just a future hope. It is also a present reality.

With such an immensity of love lavished upon us and with such things to boast of, surely it is apparent to all how superfluous is any Jewish ritual. Our peace with God, our hope of His glory, our present reconciliation, all depend upon the Cross and Resurrection of Christ. How can anyone suggest that mere circumcision could add anything to that?

---

12 Therefore, just as through one man the sin entered into the world and the death through the sin, and thus the death went through to all men, because all sinned—

13 (for until *the* Law sin was in *the* world, but sin is not charged to the account when there is no Law.

14 But the death reigned from Adam until Moses even over those who had not sinned in the likeness of Adam's transgression, who is a pattern of the *one* to come.)

The apostle continues his argument (as is apparent from the connecting **therefore**), striving to show how salvation is dependent upon Jesus Christ alone, apart from any supposed necessity of circumcision.

In this, he draws a parallel and comparison with Adam. We inherit death through Adam alone. Through that **one man, the sin** with which we are all afflicted **entered into the world** when he sinned against God in Eden, and **the death** we all experience came **through** that **sin**. Thus, that **death went through to all men, because all sinned** in Adam. We may assume that St. Paul was about to complete the parallel and add, "so in the same manner, the gift of righteousness and life came through Christ. As Adam alone led to our downfall, so Christ alone brings our restoration." But in typical fashion (for his mind overflows with new insights), Paul never completed the sentence; it is left with its conclusion to be assumed.

That is because he leaps into the midst of his own argument with another clarifying thought. He has written that **all sinned** in Adam, and in verses 13 and 14, he adds in a parenthesis the logic of how this is apparent. **Until *the* Law**, until the time of Moses, **sin was in *the* world**, but it was **not charged to the account** of sinners **when there** was **no Law**. That is, during the time **from Adam until Moses**, men still sinned, but they did not yet have the Law to define sin as sin and so warn them off. Their sin therefore was not a deliberate act of defiant rejection, as was the sin of Adam; thus it was **not charged to** their **account** or reckoned to be as serious as that first primordial act of rebellion.

Nonetheless, **death** still **reigned** over all those during the time **from Adam until Moses**, even if they **had not sinned in the likeness of Adam's transgression**. So (the argument runs), if all men received the same judgment of death as Adam did, even though they never sinned *in themselves* as he did, then obviously they must have sinned *in Adam*. That is, they were judged and sentenced to mortality not because of their own personal sins, but because of their *solidarity with Adam*. He and he alone was the source of their death. And in the same way (St. Paul means to stress), Christ and Christ alone is the source of our life. Jewish works of the Law contribute nothing. Thus Adam was **a pattern** (Gr. *tupos* or "type") of **the *one* to come**. Adam prefigured Christ in that his actions had a universal and definitive effect.

15 But the gift *is* not as the offense. For if by the
offense of the one, the many died, much more
did the grace of God and the free-*gift* in the
grace of the one Man, Jesus Christ, abound to
the many.
16 And the *free*-gift *is* not like *that which came*
through the one who sinned, for indeed the
judgment *came* from one *offense* for condemnation, but the gift *came* from many offenses
for justification.
17 For if, by the offense of the one, death reigned
through the one, much more those who receive
the abundance of grace and of the free-*gift* of
righteousness will reign in life through the One,
Jesus Christ.
18 For if through the offense of the one *there came*
condemnation to all men, thus also through
the one just-requirement there came justification of life to all men.
19 For as through the one man's disobedience
the many were appointed sinners, thus also
through the obedience of the One the many
will be appointed righteous.
20 And *the* Law sneaked-in that the offense might
grow, but where the sin grew, the grace over-
abounded,
21 that, as the sin reigned in death, thus also the
grace might reign through righteousness to
eternal life through Jesus Christ our Lord.

The apostle continues his parallel between Adam and Christ, showing that although they are alike in each being a source of universal effect for humanity, they are in other ways dissimilar.

It is true, in summary, that there is a parallelism of effect. For **through the offense of the one** (Adam), ***there came*** **condemnation to all men**, and in like manner **through the one just-requirement** or act of righteousness on the Cross (Gr. *dikaioma*), **there came justification of life to all men**. Thus, **through the one man's disobedience the many were appointed sinners** (in that they were condemned to die, and put in the same category as the sinner Adam), and **through the obedience of the One** Jesus Christ, **the many will be appointed righteous** (in that they are to be offered forgiveness and life).

Nonetheless, this parallelism of effect does not imply that the two are equal in power. It is not simply that Christ's gift of righteousness and salvation undoes the effects of Adam's sin. Rather, it brings us to a whole new level, for the power of God's grace in Christ far surpasses the power of human sin. Thus **the gift *is* not as the offense**. The gift of life (or "endowment," Gr. *charisma*) flowing from the Cross is far greater than the offense of Adam. For if by Adam's one **offense, the many died** on earth, **much more did the grace of God and the free-*gift* in the grace of the one Man, Jesus Christ, abound to the many**. For **the judgment** of God and the sentence of death for our race ***came*** **from one *offense***, resulting in **condemnation**. (A play on words in the Greek: *judgment* [*krima*] resulted in *condemnation* [*katakrima*].) Adam's single sin and definitive act of rebellion brought the catastrophe of universal death. In his case, only one offense brought death. But in the case of Christ, all the **many offenses** and sins of mankind throughout the ages are overcome by the **gift** of life flowing from His Cross and resulting in **justification** for us.

Thus, though similar to Adam's sin in having a universal effect, Christ's power is **much more** effective. Through one man, Adam, **death reigned**. If that is so, then **through the One, Jesus Christ**, how much more will we **reign in life** when we receive **the abundance of grace and of the free-*gift* of righteousness**.

Paul's point, of course, is to show how needless is the Law in all this. If Christ's power to save and give life is greater than Adam's to transmit death, then how can anyone suggest that the Jewish Law is still needed? The Jew, of course, insists that the Law was given in order to give life. Anyone can see that this is not the case and it is not needed for this. So, the Jew might ask, why was the Law given at all?

The Law **sneaked-in**, the apostle answers, **that the offense might grow**. In saying that the Law *sneaked-in* (Gr. *pareiserxomai*—the same word used in Gal. 2:4 to describe "false-brethren" infiltrating the Church's ranks), St. Paul means to show how the Law came in alongside (the literal meaning of the word) as a later insertion (almost as a kind of interloper) into the plan of God. God's plan was that those who died in Adam might be made alive in Christ. The Law was given to Israel, not in order to give life (that was for Christ to do), but to let us see the heinousness of our sins and to welcome Christ's salvation all the more. In other words, its purpose was not to be an alternative to salvation by Christ, but to complement it. It came alongside sin that sin **might grow** in men's eyes. The Law thus was not given to destroy sin, but, in a way, to undergird it. For when the Law condemns our sinful behavior, we struggle against our sins and thereby come to know the real strength of them. Our sins grow in power the more we fight against them. Only then, in the desperation of our failing fight, can we truly appreciate our need for salvation.

So the Law's function is not to eliminate sin (as the Jews thought), but on the contrary, to make it *grow*. But this does not mean the victory of sin! Rather, **where the sin grew, the grace over-abounded**. When we come to recognize the power of sin in our lives, the grace of Christ is there as well to destroy its power, bringing us cleansing, forgiveness, and life. The apostle here uses the Greek word *upereperisseusen*. He says not merely that grace "abounded" (Gr. *perisseuo*), but that it *over*-abounded (Gr. *uperperisseuo*—the same word he uses in 2 Cor. 7:4 to describe his overflowing joy at the thought of his beloved converts). By this word, he describes how Christ's grace and power flood our lives, completely ridding us of our sins. Formerly, **sin reigned** in this world, and was seen to be triumphant through the **death** that afflicted all. Now God's **grace reigns** in our lives instead. Sin's reign in us has been replaced by

☙ EXCURSUS:

On Inheriting the Sin of Adam

The concept of "original sin"—the sin of our origins, inherited from Adam—has been a vexed question in the history of the Church. In this, the Orthodox position differs somewhat from that of the Western Church, with its weighty legacy from St. Augustine of Hippo. The concept of ancestral inheritance is particularly difficult for modern man to grasp, since society has now come to think in such individualistic and atomistic terms. Persons are perceived almost entirely in terms of their isolated individuality, and the idea of inherited responsibility runs contrary to our notions of fairness. "It was Adam who sinned, not we!" we are prone to cry. "Why should God blame me for something someone else did?"

First of all, it must be stressed that the Orthodox position is that guilt before God and condemnation are indeed an individual matter. If one is judged guilty before God or damned, it will only be for sins one has knowingly and deliberately committed oneself. Unlike St. Augustine (who interpreted this passage to mean that all men were born guilty before God by virtue of Adam's sin, so that babies dying unbaptized were damned), the Orthodox Church teaches that only a willful rejection of God and His light brings damnation. One will not be damned for what another does (see Ware, *The Orthodox Church*, p. 229).

Accordingly, it is taught that all men received judgment and condemnation and were put in the category of sinners in the sense that *all men inherited Adam's mortality*. That is, they inherited not eternal *guilt*, but temporal *death*. Adam was told he would die if he rejected the way of obedience to God. Ignoring that warning, he sinned and became subject to death—and all of us inherit that sentence as well.

"But," some may still object, "why should this be? For even if we inherit not eternal guilt, but only temporal death, still we are judged for what someone else did." The force of this objection only holds if all men are thought of as individual, isolated units, with Adam as but the first in a series. But in fact, Adam was not simply the first in a series, but the source and fountain of our race. If he had persevered in his righteousness, we would have inherited his joy, authority, access to God, and immortality, regardless of our deserving and simply because we were his offspring. As it is, we inherit his loneliness, weakness, and mortality, for precisely the same reason. It is not a question of fairness, but of what it essentially means to be someone's offspring. God could have created each person individually, as He did Adam, so that no one owed anything to anyone else. He could have decided to forgo the drama of sexuality and family, so that there were no offspring. But He decided otherwise—and even in this fallen world, much of our joy comes from the two divine blessings of sexuality (that is, marriage) and family. God having decided, then, to populate the world through the production of offspring, the concept of ancestral inheritance is inevitably involved.

This is seen even in the physical world. Women who use an excess of alcohol during their pregnancy produce offspring who suffer from Fetal Alcohol Syndrome. Those who suffer from AIDS may pass that disease along to their children also. It is not a question of fairness, but of the essential inner mechanics of what it means to be offspring. The parent is the child's *source*. It is the same in the spiritual realm. In the thought of St. Paul, Adam was the primeval source for all our race. Thus he can assert that the death Adam suffered passed to all his offspring as well. It is in this sense that St. Paul speaks of all of us as having "sinned in Adam" (v. 12). Though not ourselves personally present in the Garden, we were in some sense "in the loins of our father" Adam when he was in the Garden (see Heb. 7:10), and we sinned in him in the sense that the judgment that befell him affected us also. This biblical concept of corporate personhood is wider and richer than our modern attenuated one, and it means that we share the lot of our family, tribe, nation—and even race. It does not contradict what was said above about each person ultimately being solely responsible for his or her eternal destiny. But it does mean that in this age, we are parts of a larger whole, and this larger whole has its temporal effect upon our lot in life.

These concepts of inherited judgment and corporate personhood St. Paul takes for granted—and uses them as an aid to make his main point, which is how all may inherit life from the one act of Jesus Christ. If we are to understand what he writes, we must transcend our narrow modern prejudices concerning the limits of personhood and open our minds to this ancient truth.

righteousness, and instead of being destined for death, we are to inherit **eternal life through Jesus Christ our Lord.**

§II.6 This new life means freedom from sin

The apostle has argued until now how God's righteousness and life came through faith in Christ alone, and was not dependent upon circumcision. He has argued that the Law's role in all this was not to eliminate sin but (paradoxically) to *increase* it, that there might be a greater infusion of God's grace. Paul's Judaizing opponent leaps in with an objection: What does Paul mean? Is he saying that the Christian should reject the Law and just wallow in sin, in order to maximize his experience of God's grace?

In order to refute such objections, St. Paul continues his exposition of the new life in Christ. For the Jew, rejection of the Law as central could only lead to moral anarchy. The apostle shows how this is not the case for the Christian. The Christian does not make the Law central to his life, yet he still experiences that freedom from sin which is the true goal of the Law. Through his union with Christ and his experience of His Spirit, the Christian can know the true righteousness of the children of God.

6 1 What shall we say then? Are we to remain on in the sin that grace might grow?
2 May it never be! How shall we who died to sin still live in it?
3 Or are you ignorant that all of us who have been baptized into Christ have been baptized into His death?
4 Therefore we have been co-buried with Him through baptism into death, in order that as Christ was raised from *the* dead through the glory of the Father, thus we *ourselves* might also walk in newness of life.
5 For if we have become planted-together with the likeness of His death, we shall also be *in that* of *His* resurrection,
6 knowing this, that our old man was co-crucified *with Him*, that our body of sin might be nullified, that we *ourselves* should no longer be slaves to sin,
7 for he who has died is justified from sin.
8 Now if we have died with Christ, we believe that we shall also co-live with Him,
9 knowing that Christ, having been raised from *the* dead, dies no more; death no longer is lord over Him.
10 For *what* He died, He died to sin, once for all; but *what* He lives, He lives to God.
11 Thus also you *should* reckon yourselves indeed

to be dead to sin, but alive to God in Christ Jesus.

The apostle answers the objection of the Judaizer that the implication of his teaching is that one should **remain on in the sin that grace might grow**—that one should wallow in sin so as to provide plenty of scope for the grace of God. St. Paul indignantly rejects the idea that this follows from his teaching. It is an utter impossibility! For **how shall we who died to sin still live in it?**

He here appeals to what he assumes all know (**or are** they **ignorant** of such basics?)—that **all of us who have been baptized into Christ have been baptized into His death**. Holy Baptism, as the way in which we give ourselves to Christ in faith, forms the foundation of our subsequent experience of Him. To be **baptized into** Christ means to initiate a relationship with Him and to become His disciples (just as for Israel to be "baptized into Moses" [see 1 Cor. 10:2] meant for them to begin a relationship with Moses as their teacher and leader). Through Holy Baptism, the convert expresses his faith and commitment to Christ and receives in return the washing away of sins and membership in His Body (see Acts 22:16; 1 Cor. 12:13). Thus, to be baptized means the beginning of a new union with Christ (expressed in the Greek by the preposition *eis*—baptism *into* Christ). All of this is uncontroverted. What Paul reminds us of is the implication that this union with Christ is also a union with Him *in His death*—that we have not just been baptized into Christ as our Teacher, but also **baptized into His death**.

For this sacramental union with Christ means union with Him in all that He has accomplished for our salvation. Thus we share His death, His burial, His Resurrection, His Ascension. We share His sitting on the right hand of God and His heavenly glory (see Eph. 2:6). All that He has done and experienced is for us, and He shares this sacramentally with us through baptism.

Thus **through baptism** we **have been co-buried with Him into death**. The word translated (a bit awkwardly) *co-buried* is the Greek *sunthapto* (the *sun-* prefix indicating the joint "co-" aspect of the burial). The thought is not of being buried just as Christ was, but of being buried *along with Him* and of sharing His burial. That is, through baptism we share the fullness and extremity of His death. We do not just experience and share a near-death experience, or the beginning of His dying. Rather, we fully share all the reality of His death—for He was fully dead when He was buried.

This is crucial, for to share His death means also to share His inevitable Resurrection. (His Resurrection was inevitable, since, as the Anaphora of St. Basil says, it was not possible for the Author of life to be a victim of corruption.) His death and Resurrection thus form one indivisible unity and power, for at the Cross, Christ "trampled down death by death." Thus, for us to experience one reality (His death) is to experience also the other (His new resurrection life). As we share His death, we also share the triumph over it which He experienced **through the glory** and power **of the Father** when He was **raised from *the* dead**. In His Resurrection, Christ was raised to the **newness of life** of the Age to Come, and this was so that, through baptism, **we *ourselves*** might share this life and **might also walk in newness of life.**

Baptism therefore constitutes being **planted-together with the likeness of His death**. The word translated *planted-together* is the Greek *sumphutoi*. (Its cognates are used in Matt. 15:13, where it speaks about a plant [*phuteia*] being planted [*ephuteusen*].) The idea of *sumphutos* therefore is of being co-planted, of growing together as one organic life with something else, of being inextricably joined together. In baptism, St. Paul says, we are fused together with **the likeness of His death**. That is, we are organically part of His death, sharing its exact likeness and power. (The word *likeness* here does *not* mean "like, but not the same as"; it is used as in 5:14 to mean "like in all respects, resembling and reproducing exactly.") And, since we share **the likeness of His death, we shall also** share that of **His resurrection**. The closeness with which we share His death is our assurance of sharing His life as well.

For Christ's death involved the death of sin. He did not just die—**He died to sin**, and by His death He destroyed sin's tyrannous hold over us. When Christ was crucified, He put to death the power of sin. Thus, in saying that we share His death, and that our **old**

man and life was ***co*-crucified with Him** (Gr. *sustauroo*), Paul is saying that **our body of sin** and sinful habits were **nullified** on the Cross. Thus **we *ourselves*** need **no longer be slaves of sin**. We were dead with Him—and **he who has died is justified** and freed **from sin**. (*Justified* is here used in the sense of acquitted and forgiven: the man who is acquitted of a charge is free to go—and even thus were we freed from sin. See also its use in Acts 13:39.) The apostle here points out the truism that those who have died can no longer be charged with any crime—death marks the border of sin in this world. In the same way, he says, our sharing Christ's death means that sin no longer has any hold on us.

Thus, as we share Christ's death to sin, we thereby share also His triumphant life, as we ***co*-live with Him** (Gr. *suzao*). At His Resurrection, Christ transcended death and **dies no more**, since death can no longer be **lord over Him** (Gr. *kurieuei*, cognate with *kurios*, lord). Now, Christ alone is Lord over all. He died **once for all** and now forever **lives to God**. As those who share that life now, we **also *should* reckon** ourselves **to be dead to sin, but alive to God**. We share His resurrection life now, in this age, manifesting it by our victory over sin and life of righteousness in God.

Since all this is so, how can the Judaizer say that dispensing with the Law brings slavery to sin? As those united to Christ in His death and Resurrection, we have died to sin and are alive to God. And how can those **who died to sin still live in it?**

12 Therefore do not let the sin reign in your mortal body for obeying its desires,
13 and do not present your members *as* weapons of unrighteousness to sin, but present yourselves to God as those alive from *the* dead and your members as weapons of righteousness to God.
14 For sin shall not be lord over you, for you are not under Law, but under grace.
15 What then? Shall we sin because we are not

under Law but under grace? May it never be!
16 Do you not know that to whom you present
yourselves *as* slaves for obedience, you are slaves
of the one whom you obey, either of sin for
death or of obedience for righteousness?
17 But thanks *be* to God that *though* you were
slaves of sin, you obeyed from *the* heart that
pattern of teaching to which you were delivered,
18 and having been freed from the sin, you were
enslaved to righteousness.
19 (I speak *according to* man because of the weakness of your flesh.) For just as you presented
your members *in* slavery to uncleanness and
to lawlessness for lawlessness, now thus present
your members *in* slavery to righteousness for
sanctification.
20 For when you were slaves of sin, you were free
as to righteousness.
21 Therefore what fruit were you then having in
the things of which you are now *thoroughly*
ashamed? For the end of those things *is* death.
22 But now having been freed from the sin and
enslaved to God, you have your fruit, for sanctification, and the end, eternal life.
23 For the ration-pay of sin *is* death, but the gift
of God *is* eternal life in Christ Jesus our Lord.

Having reminded us that we have been set free from sin through our baptismal union with Christ, the apostle continues to exhort us to live in that blood-bought freedom. As Christ now "lives to God," so should we (v. 11)—which means we must **not let the sin reign** in us. St. Paul refers to our **mortal body** as the arena of testing to show how weak and prone to sin all are. We have not yet entered upon the triumph and immortality of the final resurrection, but still groan in this "body of humiliation" (Phil. 3:21), subject to death and sin. Now is the time for vigilance! For in the mortal body surge powerful **desires**, lusts, and appetites, which must be controlled. Sin is pictured as a king, demanding loyal service and submission. We are not to **obey** him or submit to his reign in our bodies, carrying out his desires. We must not **present** our bodily **members** to him as **weapons of unrighteousness**, fighting for him as his loyal soldiers. On the contrary, we must do the opposite! We must **present** ourselves **to God**, our *true* King, and act as *His* soldiers, offering our members to Him as **weapons of righteousness**. Like Christ, we too have been raised by God (v. 5), and thus owe our loyal obedience to Him, not to sin. God and sin wage war against each other in this age, like two rival kings striving for control. We have been liberated from the sovereignty of sin under which we once labored—we should not present our members to him for service any longer. Sin cannot **be lord over** us or tyrannize us any more. The **Law** could not set us free from sin's thralldom, but we **are not under Law, but under grace**. And God's grace and power, experienced in baptism, has set us free from sin. Now we can fight for Him!

The voice of the Judaizer is again heard (v. 15), for he cannot imagine a life of righteousness without the Law. To be **not under Law, but under grace** could only result, he feels, in falling into an abyss of sin. Once again, the apostle strenuously denies this. **Shall we sin**, he asks, simply because we do not have the Law as our focus? **May it never be!** This is apparent by the very nature of our baptismal submission to God—for it is *the total submission of slavery*.

Here he uses an analogy from slavery—with a quick apology for referring to the exalted life of the righteous in such low terms, saying that speaking ***according to*** **man** is necessary **because of the weakness of your flesh**. The analogy may not be entirely fitting at all points, but he has to bring it down to a level that we all can understand.

He reminds us of what it means when one presents oneself **as a slave for obedience**. In that day, when one sold oneself into slavery to another person, it meant that one was totally owned by that other. The slave did not work nine to five and then have time off for himself. Rather, all the slave's time and energy were at the disposal of the master. Slavery was total by definition.

It is the same in the spiritual realm. When we formerly presented ourselves as **slaves of sin**, we served sin exclusively—resulting finally in **death**. Similarly, now that we have presented ourselves as God's slaves, devoting ourselves to **obedience** to Him (resulting finally in a life of **righteousness**), that service is total too. **Thanks *be* to God**, in our baptismal commitment to Him, we **obeyed**, from our inmost **heart, that pattern of teaching to which** we **were delivered**. Now we have been **enslaved to righteousness** (humanly speaking), serving righteousness in total and exclusive commitment—for that is what slavery means. Obviously, even without the Law, we must not live a life of sin and moral anarchy.

St. Paul's reference to the baptismal experience as being **delivered** and handed over (Gr. *paradidomi*, cognate with the noun *paradosis*, tradition) to **that pattern of teaching** is a reference to what would later be called "the rule of faith," or the Creed with its moral commentary (see 2 Tim. 1:13). It consisted of a statement of the teaching about Christ and the life of righteousness required of us if we would follow Him, a sort of elementary sketch of the Gospel. It was this early form of catechesis that Paul shared with Felix, when he discussed "faith in Christ" as entailing "righteousness, self-control, and the judgment to come" (Acts 24:24, 25). Baptism means being handed over to a life lived in conformity to that **pattern** (Gr. *tupos*, or "type"), and we have enthusiastically embraced such commitment **from *the* heart**. Now we must live it out!

St. Paul continues to encourage us in this life of holiness, which flows from our baptism (making his apology for the roughness of the analogy). In this matter, there is a clear-cut choice between two opposite and mutually incompatible alternatives—and we must choose righteousness. Formerly we **presented** our **members *in* slavery**—that is, in total submission—**to uncleanness and to lawlessness**. We lived in sexual baseness and indulgence, throwing off all moral restraint. This resulted in our spiraling ever further down into yet more **lawlessness. Now** we must **thus**, in the same way and with the same fervor, devote ourselves in **slavery** and total commitment **to righteousness**. This will result in our **sanctification** (Gr. *agiasmos*)—that is, in our transformation and glorification, as we partake of the divine nature of the Holy One (Gr. *o Agios*; see 2 Pet. 1:4).

In our former life before the Gospel, when we **were slaves of sin**, we **were free as to righteousness** and did not have to worry about fulfilling any of its demands. We could cheerfully avoid everything that the righteous were required to perform. But **what fruit** did we have when we wallowed **in *the things* of which** we **are now *thoroughly* ashamed**? (The word translated *thoroughly ashamed* is the Gr. *epaischunesthe*—for we are not just "ashamed" now of our past [Gr. *aischuno*], but *thoroughly ashamed* of it [Gr. *epaischunomai*].) That is, we could choose to serve sin, but what good or benefit did we have when we did that before? For **the end** and goal **of those things *is* death.** No wonder we left off! In our baptism we were **freed** from slavery to sin and **enslaved** instead **to God**. Now we enjoy the **fruit** we did not have before—**sanctification** and the **end** and goal that goes with it—**eternal life**. If we serve sin, there is but one **ration-pay** (Gr. *opsonia*; see its use in Luke 3:14) for the soldiers of *that* king—**death**! But God gives His own **gift** and endowment (Gr. *charisma*) to those who serve Him—**eternal life in Christ Jesus our Lord.** Here is not a ration-pay we are owed (as death is truly owed to those who serve sin), but the staggering free gift of everlasting immortality and joy, given freely as grace. This is our choice. How can we not rush to choose righteousness and life?

---

7 1 **Or are you ignorant, brothers (for I speak to those knowing *the* Law), that the Law is lord over the man for such time *as* he lives?**

2 **For the woman under-*her*-husband is bound to the living husband by *the* Law, but if the husband dies, she is abolished from the law of the husband.**

3 **So then, while the husband lives, she will be**

pronounced an adulteress if she becomes *joined*
to a different husband. But if the husband dies,
she is free from the Law—she is not an adulteress, even if *joined* to a different husband.
4 So then, my brothers, you *yourselves* also were
made to die to the Law through the body of
Christ, that you *yourselves* might become *joined*
to a different One—to Him who was raised
from *the* dead—that we might bear-fruit to
God.
5 For while we *ourselves* were in the flesh, the
passions of the sins which were through the
Law were working in our members to bear-
fruit to death.
6 But now we have been abolished from the Law,
having died to that by which we were held-
back, so that we serve *as slaves* in the newness
of the Spirit and not in the oldness of the
letter.

The apostle here continues his argument from the previous chapter, where he asserted that the reason believers can now overcome sin is that they are no longer under Law, but under grace. In this chapter, he further reflects on the nature of the Law, always with an eye on his Judaizing opponent. For this opponent asserts that the Law is eternal in application and that it will be the focus of the righteous man forever. It is meant to guide us not only in this present age, but also in the age to come.

In rebuttal, St. Paul asserts that the Law is characteristic of this age only and that it can have no eternal relevance for us in the deathless age to come. Its significance for us is bounded by this age—that is, by death. When we leave this age through death, the Law will cease to have any relevance to our continuing life, since it manifestly has to do with the social realities of this present life. Thus, the death of Christ forms the boundary of the Law, since His death and Resurrection have ushered us into the Kingdom of God and the age to come. Our baptismal participation in the death of Christ therefore means that we have transcended the Law, for through His death Christ left this age and, through our union with Him, we leave it too. This present world, bounded by death, characterized by the Law, is transcended in Christ.

St. Paul calls upon his readers to recognize this basic characteristic of the Law, saying**, Are you ignorant, brothers, that the Law is lord over the man for such time as he lives?** He speaks **to those knowing the Law**, expecting them to acknowledge its this-worldly character.

As an illustration, he gives an example, **the law of the husband** (or the teaching of the Law relating to husbands and marriage). According to the Law, **the woman under-*her*-husband** (that is, under his authority as married; the word is used in Num. 5:29) **is bound to the living husband**. That means that **while the husband lives, she will be pronounced an adulteress if she becomes *joined* to a different husband**. Thus the Law is firm and its provision secure: if she joins herself to another man, she will be **pronounced** and labeled a sinful **adulteress**—a harsh sentence indeed, leading to execution (Lev. 20:10). But see the difference that the death of her husband makes! In that case, **if the husband dies, she is abolished from the law of the husband** (*abolished* is Gr. *katergeo*, a stronger and more permanent word than merely "released"—even though it makes for awkward English—and the same word used in 2 Thess. 2:8 for the abolishing of the Antichrist). So, even if she does exactly the same thing that, before her husband's death, would have led to her execution, once that death occurs, **she is free from the Law—she is not an adulteress, even if *joined* to a different husband.** Obviously, death makes all the difference, bringing freedom from the Law. Thus, St. Paul concludes, the Law manifestly applies to this life and this age only. Death removes us from the Law's sphere of influence and jurisdiction.

And this removal through death, he argues, is what happened to us at baptism. **You *yourselves* also**, he says, **were made to die to the Law through the body of Christ, that you *yourselves* might become *joined* to a different One—to Him who was raised from**

the **dead.** Just as the woman in his illustration was once joined to her first husband and then released from that bond through death to be joined to another, so it was with us. We were once joined to the Law as to our lord and master and spiritual focus. We were released from that bond through death—not the death of the Law (for in St. Paul's thought the Law is "holy" and "spiritual" and therefore immortal; see vv. 12, 14), but rather through *our* death *to* the Law. (The parallel between us and the woman of his illustration cannot be exact.) Like the woman, having been released from the Law, we have been joined to Another—even **to Him who was raised from the dead** and who takes us beyond the boundary of death in the age to come.

The final purpose of this transcendence of the Law is not (as the Jew might fear) moral anarchy. On the contrary, once released from the Law and joined to Christ, we are to **bear-fruit to God**. Being **under grace** thus does not mean living in unrighteousness, but rather increased spiritual fruitfulness. As the Prophets predicted of the Kingdom of God, "In the days to come, Jacob will take root and will fill the whole world with fruit" (Is. 27:6). Before, we bore no fruit for God, but all our deeds were unfruitful and self-serving; now, we produce the fruit of light, in all goodness and righteousness and truth, and are useful to God and men (see Eph. 5:9, 11).

This is new, and better than anything the Law can give. **For while we *ourselves* were in the flesh, the passions of the sins which were through the Law were working in our members to bear-fruit to death.** That is, before we came to know Christ's grace, our sinful and rebellious **passions** were stirred up **through the Law**. The Greek word for *passions* is *pathemata* (often used for "sufferings," see 2 Cor. 1:6), here denoting the inner appetites and compulsions that afflict the human soul. These appetites **worked** in our **members** and manifested themselves in our bodily existence to **bear-fruit to death**. Far from the Law liberating us from the reign of sin, the Law actually aroused our sleeping passions and produced deeds that led only to death. We were not fruitful for God, but for death!

But now that we are no longer under Law but under grace, and

have been abolished from the Law and have **died to that by which we were held-back** and bound, we experience spiritual renewal and fruitfulness. The phrase *abolished from the Law* refers back to the illustration of the woman whom death released from her first husband. She was said to have been **abolished from the law of the husband.** That is, the Law relating to her marriage bond had been entirely abrogated in her case. In the same way, St. Paul now says, we Christians **have been abolished from the Law**—the Law has been entirely done away as far as we are concerned—we have transcended it completely. Formerly we were **held-back** and restrained, being subject to it. But no more. Having **died** to it through our union with Christ's death, we now **serve *as slaves*** (Gr. *douleuo*, cognate with *doulos*, "slave") **in the newness of the Spirit.**

In our old days under the Law, our service to God was **in the oldness of the letter.** That is, like this old and decaying age, our service consisted in the outward observance of ancestral religious customs. The letters of the Law that had been outwardly carved upon Moses' tablets of stone formed the limit of our spirituality. It all had to do with the merely external things of the body (see Heb. 9:10). But now we serve **in the newness of the Spirit** (Gr. *kainoteti*—not just "young and new in time" [Gr. *neos*], but "brand-new, previously unknown" [Gr. *kainos*]). The Holy Spirit within us has given us an inward renewal in which we can serve God in the freshness of the Kingdom and the age to come.

---

7 What shall then we say? Is the Law sin? May it never be! But I would not have known the sin except through *the* Law, for I would not have known desire if the Law had not said, "You shall not desire."

8 But the sin, taking an opportunity through the commandment, worked out in me all *kinds of* desire, for without *the* Law, sin *is* dead.

9 And I *myself* was once alive without *the* Law,

but when the commandment came, sin lived-
again and I *myself* died,
10 **and it was found *by* me that the command-**
ment, which was for life, this *was* for death;
11 **for the sin, taking an opportunity through the**
commandment, deceived me and, through it,
killed me.
12 **So then, the Law is holy and the command-**
ment is holy and righteous and good.

St. Paul then deals with another Jewish objection. "What does this mean?" says his opponent. "Are you saying, Paul, that **the Law is sin**?" The apostle indignantly rejects such a conclusion, saying, **May it never be!** Nevertheless, he admits that he **would not have known the sin except through *the* Law**. The Law is not sin in itself, but it does convey to him the experiential knowledge of sin. For he **would not have known** what it was to **desire** and covet (Gr. *epithumia*—the word used for "coveting" in Ex. 20:17, LXX) **if the Law had not said, "You shall not desire"** and covet.

What could this mean? Here Paul speaks autobiographically, relating the experience of every thoughtful Jew who has struggled against sin in his youth and reflected upon its internal origin. For when Paul was a young child, he was **alive without *the* Law**. It is true that he was mortal and as such had sinful passions latent within his members. Nonetheless, as one who lived in untroubled and unreflective spontaneity, he did not rebel against God—he just did what he wanted. Indeed, as a young child, he scarcely *knew* about God's demands. This is what he means by saying that he was **once alive**—not that he enjoyed immortal life as Adam did in Paradise, but that he did not experience God's condemnation of him for sin. For that condemnation and guilt only came through a deliberate breaking of the Law—which is why Paul says that **without *the* Law, sin *is* dead**.

But this time of innocence could not last. **The commandment came**. All too soon he knew that God had said, **"You shall not desire"** or covet, and then the sinful appetites that had lain dormant in him **lived-again**, springing to life, and then he **died**. As soon as God's Law said, "Don't do this!" then he was filled with **all kinds** of desire to do exactly what God had forbidden. Before this, he had the desire to covet, but this appetite was not present *as sin*. Now that he *knew* it was forbidden, he wanted it even more insistently, and what before had been present simply as a desire was now present as sin.

Thus, sin took **opportunity through the commandment** and **deceived** him. How did it deceive him? The appetite promised him happiness if he would indulge it, but when he sinned and indulged in the appetite, he found that it brought unhappiness and death. So, the final result was that the Law, which was meant to give **life** when it was obeyed, actually in this case gave **death** when it was defiantly disobeyed. The Law is not sin. But even so, though it is **holy**, and its **commandment** is still **holy and righteous and good**, it did provide the opportunity for sin to **kill** him. In Paul's experience, the Law functioned as a sort of unwilling accomplice to sin, resulting in his spiritual death. It provided the opportunity for sin, latent in his members, to rebel against God.

13 Did *that which is* good, then, become death to me? May it never be! But *rather it was* the sin—in order that it might shine *as* sin by working out death to me through *that which is* good, that through the commandment, the sin might become surpassingly sinful.
14 For we know that the Law is spiritual, but I am fleshly, sold under sin.

Once again, St. Paul's Judaizing opponent is encountered. "If sin took opportunity through the commandment to kill Paul," he objects, "then does this not mean that the Law killed him? How could that be? How could ***that which is* good** become **death** to him? Paul may confess that the Law is holy and the commandment is holy and righteous and good, but he still says that it wields death!"

In answer, the apostle is careful to identify exactly what it is that wields death—not the Law, but **the sin** that lies in his members. Paul's Jewish opponent feels that the reason God gave the Law is to eliminate sin and to give life. Paul knows that the reason God gave the Law is not to eliminate sin, but so that we could know sin for what it is and hate it. The Law is to have a didactic role, not a salvific one.

For when we see how sin can **work out death** in us even through **that which is good** (namely, **the commandment**)—then we can see how terrible sin really is. For **we know that the Law is spiritual**, whereas we ourselves are **fleshly, sold** into bondage to **sin**. That is, we know that the Law is holy, reflecting the transcendent character of the holy, mighty, and immortal God, whereas we are weak, transient, bound by our desires and the world of the senses, helpless to save ourselves. Obviously, if sin could even use something as holy as the Law to kill us, then sin must be **surpassingly sinful** indeed! Thus our experience of the Law is meant to instill in us a loathing for sin, so that it might **shine *as* sin** in our eyes. (The word translated here *shine*—Gr. *phane*—is used in Matt. 24:27 to describe the flashing of the lightning, and in Gen. 1:15 LXX to describe the stars shining in the sky. The thought is of sin appearing in its true light, being openly manifested as something utterly heinous.)

15 For that which I work out, I do not know, for I do not practice what I will, but I do the very thing I hate.

16 But if I do the very thing I do not will, I agree with the Law, that it is right.

17 But now, I *myself* no longer work it out, the sin dwelling in me.

18 For I know that nothing good dwells in me, that is, in my flesh, for to will is ready-to-hand in me, but to work out the good is not.

19 For the good that I will, I do not do, but I practice the very wickedness that I do not will.
20 But if I am doing the very thing I *myself* do not will, I *myself* am no longer the one working it out, but the sin that dwells in me.
21 I find then the law that the wickedness is ready-to-hand in me, the one who wills to do the right.
22 For I delight in the Law of God according to the inner man,
23 but I see a different law in my members, soldiering-against the law of my mind and taking me captive to the law of sin which is in my members.
24 Miserable man *am* I! Who will rescue me from the body of this death?

Exactly *how* heinous sin is can be seen by Paul's early experience of being "in the flesh," when he struggled with his "passions" (v. 5) prior to becoming a Christian. For he says **that which** he **works out** in his life, he does **not know**. He cannot fathom or make sense of it all. He does **not practice what** he wills to do, but rather **the very thing** he **hates**. He makes no move to defend himself. The Law has done its didactic work, and he **agrees with the Law** that it is **right** and good (Gr. *kalos*—the same word used in Gen. 1:4 LXX to describe the goodness of creation). It is *he* that is in the wrong—not the Law! But that being the case, it is not his true self doing it, but his fallen and false self. He does not **work it out** and do those things; rather it is **the sin that dwells in** him.

One must be clear that Paul is far from denying moral responsibility for his actions. It is, of course, he who sinned and he who will be judged for it on the Last Day. He is not denying this. The point that he makes is simply that in sinning, he is not only false to *God*, he is also false to *himself*. The real Paul—the one made in the image of God, the one who sees sin with loathing and repents with tears—this Paul is as grieved over his sinfulness as God is. This Paul **delights in the Law of God according to the inner man**. In his inmost self, he wants desperately to keep God's Law. But he sees **a different law in** his **members, soldiering-against the law of** his **mind and taking** him **captive to the law of sin which is in** his **members.**

Here he accurately describes the plight of all who have ever struggled against sinful addiction and lost. In his life, in his **flesh** and **members**, he observes a stubborn bondage and an inner traitor. It is not a matter of being burdened by one's physical body. By *flesh* (Gr. *sarx*), St. Paul does not just mean the physical body as opposed to the nonphysical soul. (He can, for example, speak of the "fleshly mind," Col. 2:18.) By *the flesh*, St. Paul means the life of the senses as it has degenerated into a state of settled rebellion against God. This attitude of rebellious sensuality is planted deeply in the human heart, poisoning personhood and working against whatever good is undertaken. Like Judas hiding in the midst of the Twelve, so this inner Judas lurks within each of us. This is what St. Paul refers to when he says **nothing good dwells in me.** In the dark parts of his personality, **that is, in** his **flesh**, there is nothing but poison. And this inner poison, **the sin dwelling in** him, is responsible for his inner struggle. **For the good that I will, I do not do, but I practice the very wickedness that I do not will.**

The rabbis of Paul's day identified the same sort of struggle in the human heart and spoke of "the evil impulse" (the *yetser hara*) with which we were born, and also of "the good impulse" (the *yetser hatob*). For them, of course, the Law was the answer. Paul knows the Law to be part of the problem, but both recognize the reality of the inner struggle. Paul's experience of the Law is also an experience of defeat. He sees and approves of the good and noble life of moral victory that God holds out before him. And too many times, he is powerless to fulfill it, despite his earnest desire. The Law of God in which he delights is opposed by the law or principle of sin, which works within him. Like a fierce-fighting and invincible enemy, this inner law **soldiers-against** him (Gr. *antistrateuomai*, cognate with *stratiotes*, "soldier") and overcomes him, **taking** him **captive** (Gr. *aixmalotizo*, cognate with *aixmalosia*, "prisoner of war"; see Num. 31:12 LXX). As a captive, he is wretched in his bondage and cries out, **Miserable man *am* I!** [a poignant cry of but three emphatic words in the Greek: *Talaiporos ego anthropos!*] **Who will rescue me from the body of this death?**

His Jewish debater points to the Law as a necessity and feels that without its centrality, there is no hope for moral victory. In reply, St. Paul relates here his own experience as a reflection of the universal plight. The Law, he says, is not only *not* the answer, it is a part of the problem! While in the flesh, his passions could not but be stirred up by the Law, that he might "bear-fruit to death" (v. 5). The Law is manifestly powerless to rescue him. From where will his salvation come?

25 **Thanks *be* to God through Jesus Christ our Lord! So then, I myself indeed with my mind serve *as a slave* the Law of God, but with *my* flesh *the* law of sin.**

8 1 ***There is* then now no condemnation to those in Christ Jesus.**

2 **For the law of the Spirit of life in Christ Jesus has set you free from the law of the sin and of the death.**

Here St. Paul reaches the climax of his argument, trumpeting out the triumphal answer to his dilemma. **Thanks *be* to God through Jesus Christ our Lord!** Jesus is the answer to his plight, and His grace the remedy for his sins. Paul sums up his plight one last time, listing the two equal contenders in the contest for our life—**the Law of God** and ***the* law of sin**—and how they divide him up, leaving him powerless and cloven in two. With his **mind** he is a willing slave to the one, but with his **flesh**, he languishes in unwilling bondage to the other. Rescue and resolution can only come through **Christ Jesus**, who introduces a third principle and power into his life: **the law of the Spirit of life. Now** that he is no longer under Law but under grace (6:14), now that he has come to be **in Christ Jesus** through holy baptism (8:1), there is **no condemnation**. That is, not only is he forgiven his sins, but he is liberated from their power and inner compulsion. Under the Law, he found himself a miserable prisoner of war and cried out, "Who will rescue me?" (7:24). In the Gospel, he has come to find that it is Christ, by the power of His **Spirit**, who has come to **set** all the prisoners **free from the law of the sin and of the death**. (The best MSS read **set *you* free**, rather than **set *me* free**, for Paul means here to make the transition from his own personal experience to that of all Christians.)

3 For what the Law was unable *to do*, weak as it was through the flesh, God *did*—sending His own Son in *the* likeness of flesh of sin and for sin, He condemned sin in the flesh,
4 that the just-requirement of the Law be fulfilled in us—those who walk not according to *the* flesh but according to *the* Spirit.

St. Paul now explains how Christ has rescued us. **The Law was unable** to rescue us, since it was **weak through the flesh**. That is, the Jewish Law was too weak to bring us victory over sin, since all it could do was simply to tell us how to behave. In our flesh, in the poisoned centers of our personality, we rebelled against what it told us. Thus **God *did*** what the Law was unable to do. He rescued us by **sending His own Son** to transform us so that **the just-requirement of the Law** might now be **fulfilled in us**. Thus the Gospel "made the Law to stand" (3:31) and established it. We have to fulfill what the Law requires of us and overcome the law of sin—however, this is accomplished not through our focus on the Law itself, but through the power of Christ.

Thus, God does not condemn *us* (v. 1)—rather, He **condemned sin**! That is, *we* are not abandoned to guilt and destruction, but instead, *sin* is the object of His wrath. Through Christ's death **in the**

flesh on the Cross, He "died to sin" (6:10), trampling down its power. Sin strives in the arena of human flesh, and it is in this same arena that Christ won the victory over it. Thus He came **for sin**—to deal with it and overcome it. The phrase translated *for sin* (Gr. *peri amartias*) is used in the Law to mean "for a sin offering" (e.g. Num. 8:8 LXX), and it is possible that is its meaning here. In that case, the apostle means that Christ came to be a sacrifice for sin.

The incarnate Christ is said here to have been **in *the* likeness** of sinful flesh. The word *likeness* here does not mean "only approximately resembling," so as to stress the *difference* of one thing from another. Rather, what is stressed is the *exact identity* between two things (see the use of this word in Phil. 2:7—Christ is "in the likeness of men" in that He *is* a man). What St. Paul means here is that Christ came as one of us. We sinful men are of **flesh**—weak, transient, mortal—and He fully shares this humanity. (This does not mean, of course, that He shares our sinfulness! Only that He shares the human nature borne by us sinners.)

5 **For those who are according to the flesh mind the things of the flesh, but those *who are* according to *the* Spirit, the things of the Spirit.**
6 **For the mind of the flesh *is* death, but the mind of the Spirit *is* life and peace,**
7 **because the mind of the flesh *is* enmity to God, for it does not submit itself to the Law of God—indeed, neither is it able,**
8 **and those who are in *the* flesh are not able to please God.**

This victory and fulfillment of the Law's requirement presupposes that we "walk not according to the flesh but according to the Spirit" (v. 4). Our victory is not automatic; nor does it happen without our own effort in putting "to death the [evil] practices of the body" (v. 13).

For there are two types of people, and St. Paul puts them in stark opposition to challenge his hearers to choose between them: **those who are according to the flesh** (the worldlings) and **those who are according to the Spirit** (the Christians). (The apostle for now leaves out of the reckoning both the pious Jew and the righteous Gentile.) Those who are **according to the flesh** know only the fleshly, physical existence. They live in enslavement to their own sensual desires and selfishness; they **mind** (Gr. *phroneo*) and are absorbed in **the things of the flesh**. Their whole world, their entire focus, is in things that will perish, such as money, sensual gratification, reputation, wealth. The **mind**, attitude, and striving (Gr. *phronema*) set on these lead only to **death**. Obviously, Paul's hearers should not "walk according to the flesh" (v. 4)!

They are called to another way—to walk **according to the Spirit**. Those who are **according to the Spirit** are those who are born of the Spirit and live only because God has brought them to spiritual life. They live in reliance upon the Spirit's power and choose to mind **the things of the Spirit**, cultivating the Spirit's fruit (Gal. 5:22, 23, 25). Their focus is on God and how to please Him. The **mind** and striving after these lead to **life and peace**. Here is the true fulfillment of the Law!

They must then strive to avoid the mind of the flesh. It cannot lead to the life and peace they desire, for it **is enmity to God**. Such an attitude is in implacable hostility to God and His rule over the human heart. Such a mind **does not submit itself to the Law of God—indeed, neither is it able** to do so. It is locked in powerlessness, unable to break out of its hopeless rebellion. The one living thus is **not able to please God**. To **please God** (Gr. *Theo aresai*) means to win the smile of divine approval and His blessing (see Balak's attempt to please God and win His help by offering sacrifice in Num. 23:27 LXX). Those worldlings, therefore, can never know the life and peace God gives to those who please Him.

9 **You *yourselves*, though, are not in *the* flesh, but**
in *the* Spirit, if indeed *the* Spirit of God dwells

> **among you. But if anyone does not have *the* Spirit of Christ, he is not of Him.**
> **10 If Christ *is* among you, though the body *is* dead through sin, yet the Spirit *is* life through righteousness.**
> **11 But if the Spirit of *the One* who raised Jesus from *the* dead dwells among you, He who raised Christ Jesus from *the* dead will give-life also to your mortal bodies through His indwelling Spirit among you.**

St. Paul emphasizes to his hearers (the **you** is emphatic in the Greek) that this fearful fate is far from them. They **are not in the flesh, but in the Spirit**, with the obligation to mind the things of the Spirit. This is apparent because **the Spirit of God dwells among** them.

In asserting that they are no longer in the flesh but in the Spirit, the apostle appeals to their experience as a church community. It is as a community that the Spirit of God is experienced as working in power **among** them (Gr. *en umin*). This preposition *en* is very elastic in usage. It can mean "inside" (such as the apostles being "*inside* the Temple," Acts 5:42). Or it can mean "among" (such as Paul being *among* those of Rome during his visit, 1:12). It is this second meaning that predominates here, since the apostle is appealing to their corporate experience. (Obviously, these two meanings—"inside" and "among"—shade into one another in this case: the Spirit is *among* them corporately because He is also *inside* each of them individually.)

Because this Spirit is sent by Christ into their hearts at baptism (see Acts 2:33) and because the Spirit always exalts Christ as Lord (see John 16:14), this experience of having the Spirit of God among them is also an experience of having **Christ among** them. It is important to recognize that St. Paul is not writing a systematic theology or instructing his readers in doctrine so much as he is reminding them of their own life. Through the fervency of their worship, through their prophecy, through their knowledge of healings and exorcisms, they know that the Spirit of God dwells among them and Christ is in their midst. The apostle is appealing to their own undeniable experience as a gathered church.

There can be no exceptions. This obligation that comes from being **in the Spirit** is not only upon the more mature Christians, with the newer converts being exempt. They are *all* to strive to mind the Spirit. No one can say that he is not a part of that Spirit-indwelt Body, for **if anyone does not have *the* Spirit of Christ, he is not of Him**. That is, anyone who claims to belong to Christ obviously therefore also has the Spirit of Christ. To be **of Him**—and they all acknowledge that they are of Him—means they must have received Christ's Spirit as well. The apostle here appeals to a tautology—just as everything has its own characteristic "spirit," so it is apparent that to be "of" something means to partake of that "spirit." If they then are **of Christ**, they must have His **Spirit** too—and therefore have the Spirit of God.

(It may be noted in passing that **the Spirit of God** is equated here with **the Spirit of Christ** because, in the experience of the Church, the Spirit of God is given through discipleship to Christ. St. Paul is not speaking of the eternal origins of the Holy Spirit, nor does this verse have anything to do with the later *filioque* controversy.)

If all this is true, St. Paul continues, then they have divine **life** by **the Spirit** to overcome the law of sin and death—for this victory over sin is what he has been discussing since the beginning of chapter 6. The apostle tells them that though their **body** may be **dead** and mortal **through sin**, heading toward the final earthly dissolution that is the lot of us all (see 5:12), nevertheless, **the Spirit** within them **is life** and triumphant over the forces of sin and death **through righteousness**. (The **Spirit** mentioned here is obviously the Holy Spirit, as consistent with the use of the word until now, and not the human spirit. Only the Holy Spirit can be truly described, not just as "alive," but as **life**.)

It was by **the Spirit** that God **raised Christ Jesus from *the* dead** in an act of eschatological power, and if this same Spirit **dwells** (Gr. *oike*) **among** the Church, God will **give-life** also to them, even as they live in their **mortal bodies**. Those bodies may indeed be **dead through sin** and mortal. But even so, they will experience the same death-shattering power that raised Christ Jesus from the dead. This is what it means to have God's ***in*dwelling Spirit** (Gr. *enoikoun*) among them. That Spirit also dwells inside each of them, giving life, overcoming sin and death.

Through their baptism, then, each of them has been "baptized into Christ's death" (6:3) and shares in His own death to sin. Through that death Christ offered Himself as a sacrifice "for sin" (8:3), that they might become God's sons. In baptism, as God's sons, they received the Holy Spirit, who made Christ's death to sin a power in their own lives, so that "the law of the Spirit of life set them free from the law of sin and death" (8:2). In all this mighty deliverance, it is apparent that the Law has no role! How then can the Judaizers try to make it central to living the Christian life?

12 So then, brothers, we are debtors, not to the
flesh, to live according to the flesh—
13 (for if you are living according to the flesh, you
are about to die, but if by *the* Spirit you put to
death the practices of the body, you will live).
14 For as many as are led by *the* Spirit of God,
these are sons of God.

The apostle here reaches his conclusion, for which he has been preparing since beginning to argue in 6:1 that new life in Christ means freedom from sin. As those who have been "set free" (v. 2), we are no longer **debtors** to our **flesh**. For debt brings its own bondage, and the one who owes something to another is tied to him while the debt lasts. He cannot do whatever he wants; the holder of the debt has veto power over all the debtor's plans. Formerly we were **debtors to the flesh** and were compelled to **live according to the flesh**, carrying out the will of the one who held our debt. But no more! Now we need **live according to the flesh** no longer.

St. Paul is about to finish his sentence in verse 12 by saying that we are now debtors to the Spirit. But with his customary creative impulsiveness, he interrupts his thought to add a parenthesis, explaining how crucial it is not to live as debtors to the flesh, and he never finishes his sentence. The inferred sense of the rest of the thought, however, is clear enough.

In that parenthesis, he explains how this liberation from the flesh is truly our salvation, for to live in the flesh means to hover on the brink of death. Those who do so are **about to die**, facing certain doom. Here he employs a paradox: If you embrace life in the flesh, you will die, but if you embrace death by the Spirit, you will live! It is as the Lord said: "Whoever wishes to save his life will lose it, but whoever loses his life for My sake, he is the one who will save it" (Luke 9:24). **By** the power of ***the* Spirit**, they should **put to death the practices of the body**. That is, relying upon the law of the Spirit of life (8:2), they should reckon themselves dead (6:11) to all those sinful things which were once their lifestyle. All acts of sexual "uncleanness," all moral "lawlessness" (6:19), the whole life of self-absorbed search for pleasure, must all be forsaken. Doubtless there may be an inner struggle, for no living thing is easily **put to death**. Nevertheless, they must set their face ruthlessly against these practices, which will kill them. Only thus can they **live**. They should not be deceived—only **as many as are led by *the* Spirit of God** along this path of righteousness are **sons of God**. (The force of the Greek for *these are sons of God* is "these *and no others* are the sons of God.") No one who refuses to follow the Spirit on this way of asceticism, relentlessly pursuing righteousness, can call God his father.

15 For you have not received a spirit of slavery again *leading us* to fear, but you have received a Spirit of adoption-as-sons, in whom we cry out, "Abba! Father!"

16 The Spirit Himself co-witnesses to our spirit that we are children of God,

> 17 **and if children, heirs also—indeed heirs of God, and co-heirs of Christ—if yet we co-suffer *with Him* that we also may be co-glorified *with Him*.**

But (St. Paul assures us again—see his assurance in v. 9) *we* are truly His sons, and as such can cry out boldly in prayer. Here again he appeals to our liturgical experience. In baptism, we did **not receive a spirit of slavery**, leading us to servile **fear**. We **received a Spirit of adoption-as-sons**, leading us to **cry out, "Abba! Father!"**

The lowliness of the Law is here contrasted with the high and holy boldness of Gospel sonship. Under the Law, man had to cover his face before the Lord (see 2 Cor. 3:12f). This lowliness and inhibited access was characteristic of slavery, for slaves did not have the boldness to approach the master unbidden, but remained in fear and at a respectful distance until called. Since the Roman Christians have been baptized, their worship has nothing of this former experience of timidity. Rather, they now enjoy freedom of access to God, approaching Him as boldly as sons approach their own father. In baptism, they received the Spirit, and their post-baptismal worship is characterized by filial familiarity and boldness before God. In their liturgy together, they **cry out, "Abba! Father!"**—this double invocation indicating the intensity of their desire for Him (even as little children call out, "Papa! Papa!").

The word translated *cry out* is the Greek *krazo*, meaning "to shout with a loud voice, to scream." It is the word used for the shrieking of the demoniac (Mark 5:5) as well as for the loud voice of the Lord in the Temple, when He raised His voice to make Himself heard (John 7:28). Here it indicates the loud and fervent prayers of the liturgical assembly, in which the faithful address God as Father (expressed today also in the Church's use of the "Our Father"). (The use of the original Aramaic *Abba*—along with *Maranatha* in 1 Cor. 16:22—seems to represent a direct import from the Palestinian church into the liturgical life of the Gentile churches.) Here is no faint or timid approach, but an exuberant and confident access to the Most High! Such confidence can only come from sons who know that they stand before their own Father.

St. Paul points to the liturgical experience of the Church as evidence of our sonship. We are truly God's sons, having received **adoption-as-sons** in baptism and having been given the Spirit as befits sons (see Gal. 4:6). So important is this adoption that **the Spirit Himself** within each of us, He and no other (the Greek is emphatic), **co-witnesses to our spirit that we are children of God**. That is, the fervency of our filial worship, in which we cry out, "Father! Father!" from the depths of our **spirit**, witnesses that we are truly the **children of God**. The Church witnesses to us as being God's children (by including us in the post-baptismal eucharistic meal) and **the Spirit** confirms this also, by **co-witnessing** deep in our hearts (Gr. *summartureo*; the *co-* aspect is expressed in the *sum-* prefix).

This is the exalted privilege to which the Gospel admits us (and to which the Law never could)—that of being the **children of God**, cared for by Him as a father cares for His very own. (The designation *sons* [Gr. *uioi*] speaks of how Christians—regardless of gender—inherit all the authority and wealth of our heavenly Father, for in St. Paul's culture, it was the sons on whom this right devolved. The designation *children* [Gr. *tekna*] speaks of how we enjoy His loving protection and care.)

But there is more. Not only are we **children**, but **heirs also**. Since we are His own offspring, we will inherit all the joy and glory in the cosmos. "All things belonged to them" (1 Cor. 3:22). Everything belongs to **God** the Father, who gives all to His eternal Son **Christ**, who is therefore the Heir of all—yet this He freely shares with us! We are therefore **heirs of God** and **co-heirs of Christ**, sharing with our Lord Jesus the glory of the age to come. Here is the full and final meaning of our sonship—to inherit all the earth.

Yet, if we would be **co-heirs of Christ**, we must enter into our inheritance as He did His—through suffering. If we would be **co-glorified** in the age to come, then we must also **co-suffer** with Him in this present age. (We are said to **co-suffer** [Gr. *sumpasxo*]—through our sufferings in the world, we share and have communion with our Lord's suffering on the Cross.) Indeed, the lot of the sons of God in this world is the Cross. The world persecuted the Lord, and it will persecute us (John 15:20). Only by steadfastly enduring this persecution and keeping the Faith can we enter into our final and glorious inheritance. We will be **co-glorified** with Him (Gr. *sundoxaso*) in that the very same glory with which Christ was glorified by the Father at His right hand is what He will share with us. It is not just that He will give us glory too. Rather, we will be glorified with *the very glory of Christ.* Here is theosis indeed!

§II.7 We must persevere through suffering to share Christ's glory

Having said that the Roman Christians are now, through baptism alone, the children of God and therefore the heirs of God, St. Paul says also that they must first suffer before entering into their inheritance.

This seems to be a contradiction. If they are even now the children and offspring of God, why should they have to suffer? The lowliness and humiliation involved in persecution seems to run counter to their glorious status as God's sons. Perhaps their suffering means they are not yet sons of God after all. Maybe—as the Judaizers say—they also need to be circumcised.

In answer, the apostle says that, though they are God's sons now (v. 15), yet the fullness of their sonship is yet to be revealed and manifested. Later, at the Lord's Coming, will be the time for glory. Now, in this age, is the time for waiting and for perseverance—and for suffering.

❧ ❧ ❧ ❧ ❧

18 For I reckon that the sufferings of this present time *are* not worth *comparing* with the glory that is about to be revealed to us.

19 For the earnest-expectation of the creation awaits the revelation of the sons of God.

20 For the creation was submitted to uselessness not voluntarily, but because of Him who submitted it, in hope

> **21 that the creation itself also will be freed from the slavery of corruption into the freedom of the glory of the children of God.**
> **22 For we know that the whole creation co-groans and co-travails until now.**
> **23 And not only *this*, but also ourselves, having the first-fruits of the Spirit, even we ourselves groan in ourselves, waiting for *the* adoption-as-sons, the redemption of our body.**

In speaking of the **sufferings** which we must endure, St. Paul first assures us that these are **not worth *comparing* with the glory** that is soon to be revealed to us. As he wrote to the Corinthians, compared with the staggering burden of joy that will be revealed to us and in us, all our present suffering is but a momentary lightness (2 Cor. 4:17). Our hearts should not tremble when the persecutor approaches, nor should our soul draw back from faithfulness! The glory of the age to come will be more than worth the present hour of trial.

Indeed, **the earnest-expectation** of all the **creation** waits for that glory and the time when we will be **revealed** as **the sons of God**. Our sonship is the hidden secret of the world, and our royal status, the cosmic mystery. Now we live incognito and the world does not recognize us as God's sons. Rather, the world takes us for slaves and submits us to indignities, heaping the abuse of persecution upon us. But our sonship will be revealed one day, when the Lord returns, and all of creation cherishes that revelation as its **earnest-expectation**. The single Greek word translated here *earnest-expectation—apokaradokia*—literally indicates a straining forward with outstretched head, as crowds watching a race would stand craning their necks to catch a sight of the distant runners. St. Paul uses it here to show the intensity of longing with which the whole of creation **awaits** and anticipates the cosmic revelation of our sonship.

For that revelation represents its own glorification too. The creation, which was placed under the care and protection of Adam and which fell along with him (see Gen. 3:17f), was **submitted to uselessness not voluntarily, but because of Him who submitted it**. That is, sharing the primordial curse upon Adam, the created world and environment was enslaved by the will of God to futility, vanity, and entropy. Meant to share all the nobility and glory of its lord, Adam, it now suffers **the slavery of corruption**. That death and decay rule unchallenged in nature was not its original design. It did not embrace such slavery *voluntarily*, as the expression of its own original nature. Rather, this is the result of sin.

But this suffering is not to last forever. Rather, creation was submitted to slavery **in hope**. It is given the certainty that its slavery will end one day and that it will inherit the glorious **freedom** that belongs to **the children of God**. Like us, it now suffers as a slave, but one day it will be free! For now, however, all the creation **co-groans and co-travails** with the pangs of childbirth. Like the groaning complaint of the wretched poor who suffer oppression (Gr. *stenazo*; see the use of the cognate noun *stenagmos* in Ps. 12:5 LXX), the world groans and cries to God for deliverance. Like a woman suffering the pains of childbirth, the creation impatiently waits for its promised goal. (The words are used with the prefix *co-* to express the Greek *sum-* prefix [Gr. *sustanezo* and *sunodino*], I suggest, to show how creation groans and labors *along with us*.)

Creation has to endure a time of suffering before entering into its promised glory. And it is the same with us. Just as creation groans with suffering as it waits for sonship to be revealed (v. 19), so we also **groan in ourselves** as we **wait** for it (v. 23). In baptism, we received **the first-fruits of the Spirit**. That is, just as the first-fruits are harvested with joy as the token of later receiving the whole crop, so our present reception of the Spirit is the promise and token that later our **adoption-as-sons** will be complete. It is true that we are now God's adopted sons (v. 14). But our adoption to sonship, begun in baptism, is also a process, and this process will not be fulfilled until the **body** is finally redeemed at the resurrection. At this time, our physical body is under the sway of death, and that debt to mortality must be paid (see v. 10). Later, we will be fully bought back from death and redeemed. Then our sonship will be complete. Now, like the rest of creation which **co-groans** with us, we groan and wait.

> ❧ ❧ ❧ ❧ ❧
>
> **24 For in hope we have been saved—but hope *that is* seen is not hope, for why does anyone also hope for what he sees?**
> **25 But if we hope for what we do not see, with perseverance we wait for it.**

For this is what it means to have been saved **in hope**. Creation was submitted to slavery "in hope" of its eventual release (vv. 20, 21), and we share that condition. **Hope**, of course, does not imply doubt as to the final outcome, like a kind of sanctified optimism. It embraces certainty of expectation. But it is the certainty of *future realities*. Or, as the apostle writes, **hope *that is* seen** and realized is, by definition, **not hope**—for **why does anyone also hope for what he sees?** That is, if one already possesses something, he no longer has to hope for it. But now, in fact, we **hope for what we do not see** or possess, and so **with perseverance we wait for it**. It is because of the nature of our salvation as *the hope of future glory* that we must wait.

This **perseverance** implies perseverance in the midst of suffering. It is not just a passive and easy waiting, like marking time in a waiting room. Rather, it is the active and difficult waiting that comes with the endurance of suffering. It is the waiting of the arena, of the prison cell, of exile. Suffering will try to turn us away from Christ and discourage us. It will attempt to drive us back to the world and to the mind of the flesh, depriving us of our final sonship. But we are to resist that discouragement. We are to persevere and not give up our hope of glory.

> ❧ ❧ ❧ ❧ ❧
>
> **26 And in the same way the Spirit also co-helps our weakness, for we do not know what to pray**

> ***as we* ought to, but the Spirit Himself earnestly-**
> **appeals for us with unspoken groans,**
> 27 **and He who examines the hearts knows what**
> **the mind of the Spirit *is*, that He appeals for**
> **the saints according to God.**

Once more the apostle hastens to reassure us. We are not to be abandoned in our **weakness** and left to persevere by our own strength alone. Just as the creation groans with us, crying to God for deliverance, and as we ourselves also groan, crying for our final redemption, so **in the same way, the Spirit** within us also groans to God.

In doing this, He **co-helps** us in the **weakness** we experience in persecution. When our strength begins to fail and our fervor wanes, the Spirit we have received comes to take our part. (Once again, the prefix *co-* is attached to the Greek *sunantilambanomai*, indicating how the Spirit adds His strength to ours.) In the midst of our peril and confusion, we **do not know what to pray**. We **ought** to continue praying with fervor, manifesting the **mind of the Spirit** (see v. 6). But persecution works to discourage that, silencing our groans and our ceaseless cry for vindication (see Luke 18:1, 7). It is then, when persecution cools our fervor, that **the Spirit Himself earnestly-appeals** for us, working in our hearts and generating **unspoken groans**, the wordless outstretching of the soul toward God.

These renewed groans are the fruit of the Spirit's **earnest-appeal** and intercession. (The word here translated *earnestly-appeals* is the Greek *uperentugxavo*. The *uper-* prefix here indicates an intensive and is used to show the intensity of the Spirit's intercession. He does not simply "appeal" and intercede—Paul says here that He *earnestly* intercedes.)

The Spirit within thus undertakes to bear up the flagging believer, causing him to groan and cry out to God from his place of exile on earth. The suffering of tribulation may cause him to forsake his heavenly homeland and feel himself at home in his place of exile. With the Spirit's help, the believer is restored to his original zeal and cries out for God to rescue him and set him free. Just as the Spirit co-witnessed to his spirit that he was a true child of God, causing him to cry out, "Abba! Father!" (vv. 15, 16), so in his time of weakness He prays within him, causing him to groan to God.

God the Judge, the One who **examines the hearts** (see 1 Chr. 28:9; Rev. 2:23), knows when **the mind of the Spirit** is thus instilled in us. The term *the mind of the Spirit* is the same used in 8:6, indicating the attitude and mindset of the believer, as he focuses upon spiritual things. It is this **mind** and attitude (Gr. *phronema*) that the Spirit instills in him. By His help given to the believer in his weakness, the Spirit prays in him, generating His own mindset and zeal, which groans to God. The One who will judge us, searching out our inner motives on the Last Day, recognizes with approval this inner disposition, for it is the Spirit's inner **appeal** and intercession **according to God**. These inner strivings will be acceptable to the Judge because the Spirit inspires them according to the divine will.

In writing of the inner intercession of the Spirit, the apostle writes of what the Christians can know and experience. That is, he is not writing to explain abstruse theoretical things that are hidden from our knowledge. He does not say that, though we can have no actual experience of it, the Spirit is in fact interceding for us. Rather, as in everything else he writes, St. Paul refers to what Christians can directly undergo in our lives. Thus he refers to what happens to us in times of persecution—to the acknowledged reality that when we are reviled for the Name of Christ, the Spirit of glory and of God rests upon us in power (see 1 Pet. 4:14). Indeed, the constant experience of the Church is that persecution causes the Spirit's flame to burn more brightly in the believer. When we are struck with persecution, the Spirit helps us in our weakness, manifesting Himself in our hearts with more intense groaning and fervor.

Thus St. Paul does not write here of a merely theoretical ministry of the Spirit. Rather, as the Christians strive to wait with perseverance (v. 25), they can know the help and strengthening of the Spirit. By His assistance, they are empowered to join the rest of creation, with unspoken groans in their hearts, lifting up their souls to God and crying for freedom.

28 And we know that to those who love God, all things co-work for good, to those who are called according to *His* purpose,
29 because whom He foreknew, He also predestined *to be* conformed to the image of His Son, that He might be *the* Firstborn among many brothers;
30 and whom He predestined, these He also called, and whom He called, these He also justified, and whom He justified, these He also glorified.

Corresponding to God's knowledge of us (in the previous verse), St. Paul then mentions our knowledge of Him. God knows the mind of the Spirit in us, and we know that **all things co-work for good, to those who are called** in baptism, **according to** God's **purpose** proclaimed in the Gospel. St. Paul continues his discourse about the Christians having to suffer before being glorified. This suffering should not discourage us, he says, for **to those who love God**, even this suffering, along with **all things**, can only **co-work for good**. Persecution should therefore not be feared, for it can only end in good and beneficial things for us. Such suffering does not mean that we have been cut off from God's care and love. God continues in His determination to bring us to glory—even though the path be the way of the Cross that Christ walked. Such things need to be addressed, for however one may theorize while in peace, the experience of suffering often causes one to doubt the goodness and care of God.

The apostle here steps back from the stage of history to survey God's Gospel purpose from eternity past to the age to come. Before we were born, he says, God **foreknew** us (Gr. *proginosko*). The *fore-* prefix (Gr. *pro-*) expresses that God not only cares for us in this life, but that His purposes embraced us before the world was made. That is, before anything had come to exist, He had determined that all those He **foreknew** would be penitent of heart were to share this glorious fate—namely, that they were to be **conformed to the image of His Son**. This is His predestination—not the individual's salvation or damnation, but the determination that all who shall be saved will have that glory. The Jews thought that the messianic glory was that they would be exalted politically among the nations. This is not the messianic glory that God planned for those He foreknew would be tender of heart and faithful. Rather, they were to share the very glory of the Son of God, so that He **might be *the* Firstborn among many brothers**. All that Christ was by nature was to be given to them by grace.

Moreover, all those whom He foreknew and **predestined** (or marked out in advance) to this glory, He also **called** through the proclamation of the Gospel, inviting them to share Christ's sonship. These whom He called, He also **justified**, forgiving, washing, and cleansing them in baptism, separating and sanctifying them from the world (see 1 Cor. 6:11). These He also **glorified**—beginning that process of theosis whereby they are to be changed from glory to glory (see 2 Cor. 3:18)—a process which is not to cease until they have been fully conformed to the glorious image of the Son of God in the age to come. God is thus resolved that those whom He loves in Christ shall not be separated from Him by any cruel thing in this world. He foreknew their faith from ages past and will lead them to their promised glory in Christ. How can they fear that suffering means God no longer cares for them?

(In all the foregoing, St. Paul is of course speaking to the trembling hearts of those who fear that suffering can somehow separate them from the love of God, and therefore he speaks only words of assurance. The free-will and fate of those who, having been called and justified, then apostatize from their calling and turn back from their glorious destiny is not here in view.)

31 What then shall we say to these *things*? If God *is* for us, who *is* against us?

**32 He who indeed did not spare His own Son,
but delivered Him up for us all, how will He
not also with Him give us all things?
33 Who will accuse God's chosen? God *is the One*
who justifies—
34 who is the one condemning? Christ Jesus *is He
who* died, rather who was raised, who is at *the*
right hand of God, who also appeals for us.
35 Who shall separate us from the love of Christ?
Shall tribulation, or anguish, or persecution,
or famine, or nakedness, or danger, or sword?
36 As it is written, "For Your sake we are put to
death all day; we were reckoned as sheep of
slaughter."
37 But in all these things we resoundingly-
conquer through Him who loved us.**

The apostle reaches his jubilant climax of assurance in the face of suffering. When we think of **these *things***, how can we fear persecution? For **if God is for is, who** can be **against us**? (The Greek is more triumphantly terse, consisting of seven short words, like a battle-cry on a banner: *Ei o Theos uper emon, tis kath'emon?*) The mighty, invincible, and infinite Deity, the Ruler of All, is our helper. What can puny man do to counter and thwart His matchless wisdom and might (see Ps. 118:6)?

The irrefutable evidence of God's care and goodwill is that He **indeed did not spare** even **His own Son, but delivered Him up** for us all. If He is willing to dare even these lengths for our salvation, how can we imagine He would abandon us now? Rather, **will He not also with Him give us all things?** (*Give* is Gr. *charizomai*, meaning "to bestow freely as a gracious gift"; see *charis*, grace.) God has already generously given His Son. Having given the greatest gift possible, is it likely God would then become stingy? After such a Gift, what are **all things** in comparison?

St. Paul, filled with the fury of triumph, looks around to see if any dare oppose such divine generosity. Where are the Judaizers now? Where are their bold assertions that the Gentiles cannot be saved without circumcision and the Law? **Who will accuse God's chosen?** Will they? **God *is the One* who justifies—who is the one condemning?** In baptism, God pronounced us forgiven. Where are these lawyers and scribes who would overturn the verdict of the Most High? They may oppose Paul as much as they like. But it is **Christ Jesus**, the One **who died**—more than that, the One **rather who was raised**, and who has been exalted so as to sit in power **at *the* right hand of God**, ruling the universe with Him—this is the One **who appeals** and intercedes for the baptized. Are the Judaizers prepared to oppose Him too? Christ intercedes with the Father for our pardon and forgiveness. Do the Judaizers think to correct even Him—to make His intercession ineffectual?

Obviously, St. Paul's hearers have nothing to fear from suffering. It is not a sign that God does not accept them or that they have been separated from the Lord's favor. Indeed, **who** can possibly **separate us from the love of Christ?** Can **tribulation, or anguish, or persecution, or famine, or nakedness, or danger, or sword**? Given Christ's sovereignty over all the world and His sitting at the right hand of God, none of these things can happen apart from Him, nor cancel out His care. Whatever hardship or suffering we have to endure on the way to our final glory, the Lord will turn into victory. Our suffering does not mean God has abandoned us for not following Him. Rather, our situation is the same as that of the Psalmist of old, who was persecuted *precisely because* he followed God. **As it is written** (Ps. 44:22 LXX), **"For Your sake we are put to death all day; we were reckoned as sheep of slaughter."**

In **all these things**, all these experiences of suffering and distress, we **resoundingly-conquer through** Christ **who loved us** and watches over us. The verb translated here *resoundingly-conquer* is the Greek *upernikao*, with the *uper-* prefix being intensive. The thought here is not of simply surviving sufferings and coming out as victors. Rather, it is of gloriously triumphing in sufferings, strengthened through Christ who loved us. Our sufferings will serve only to work together for our good (v. 28) and provide us with radiant and eternal crowns. Even as the Lord's Cross is also His glorification (John 13:31), so also our sufferings will be our glory and a source of our joy on the Last Day.

38 **For I am persuaded that neither death, nor life,
nor angels, nor principalities, nor things
present, nor things to come, nor powers,**
39 **nor height, nor depth, nor any other creature,
shall be able to separate us from the love of
God which *is* in Christ Jesus our Lord.**

The apostle concludes all his exhortation (begun in 1:16, speaking about his Gospel and its implications) with a final cry of dogmatic defiance, cast like a challenge in the teeth of the world. **I am persuaded**, he says, that nothing—absolutely nothing—can ever separate the faithful **from the love of God which *is* in Christ Jesus our Lord**. The love of God revealed in the Gospel must triumph over all else—over suffering and slanders, over excommunications by Jews and persecutions by pagans (see Luke 21:12).

The world Paul and his hearers knew was, for them, a vaster and more varied one than the mapped and global village we know today. It was a universe crammed with unseen secrets and hidden mysteries, with frightening forces and supernatural dangers. This is reflected in some of the apocalyptic literature then current, such as the *Book of Enoch*, which was popular in that day and quoted in the New Testament (Jude 14, 15, quoting Enoch 1:9). The hidden dangers that haunted the world, the secret springs of supernatural power, are mentioned in that book and may be quoted here as a sample of the menacing possibilities that threatened any seeking to reach heaven.

In the *Book of Enoch*, the hero Enoch is given an angelic tour through earth and Sheol, the land of the dead. "They took and brought me," he says, "to a place in which there were those like flaming fire. I came to a river of fire. I saw the mouths of all the rivers of the earth. I saw the treasuries of all the winds and I saw the cornerstone of the earth which bears it and the firmament of heaven. I saw the paths of the angels; I saw at the end of the earth the firmament of the heaven above. I proceeded and saw a place which burns day and night, where there is a mountain which reaches to heaven like the throne of God. Beyond these mountains is a region, the end of the great earth: there the heavens are completed. And I saw a deep abyss, with columns of heavenly fire, beyond measure alike towards the height and towards the depth. And beyond that abyss I saw a place which had no firmament above and no earth beneath, but it was a waste and horrible place. And the angel said to me, 'This has become a prison for the stars and the host of heaven. Here stand the angels who have defiled mankind'" (ch. 18).

It is considering the panorama of such possibilities that the apostle affirms that nothing—not even such staggering powers as these—can come between the faithful and their Lord. There is nothing we can encounter in either **death** and Sheol or in this **life** on earth that can place us beyond Christ's protection and love. Neither the hosts of **angels** on high, nor the demonic **principalities** and **powers** that rule this earth (see the use of the terms in 1 Cor. 15:24) can hinder us. Neither the **things present** in this age nor the **things to come** in the future age have any power over us. Neither anything in the **height** of the firmament nor in the **depth** of the abyss can harm us. Indeed, no **other creature** at all has power **to separate us** from God's love, which we have come to experience in the Gospel of **Christ Jesus our Lord**.

If in that love we are safe and secure from all the vast array of creation's supernatural wonders and dangers, how much more are we safe from mere earthly suffering! Through baptism and our faith alone, Paul proclaims, we are made God's sons. Soon we will enter the fullness of our sonship. The path of suffering we must tread on the way need not make us tremble.

Notes for Section II:

____

____

Notes for Section II:

ꕥ III ꕥ

THE ROLE OF ISRAEL (9:1—11:36)

Having dealt at length with the Gospel that he will preach at Rome and having defended it from the objections of the Judaizers, St. Paul begins a new topic—defending himself from Jewish accusations of fundamental disloyalty to Israel. For as far as the Judaizers and all his fellow Jews are concerned, Paul is simply a renegade from the Law. Moreover, it seems to them that he is denying one of the basic tenets of his ancestral faith, that of the calling and election of Israel. For if the Gentiles are to be included and saved without becoming circumcised Jews, then what is the point of God's calling Israel? Paul seems to his Jewish countrymen to be repudiating their entire sacred history. More than that, in his opposition to them, it seems that he is actually anti-Israel, calling down God's wrath upon them and delighting in their harm (see Acts 13:45–51; 1 Thess. 2:15, 16). St. Paul emphatically denies that this is so. He does *not* delight in their downfall, nor does he deny that Israel is chosen from among the nations to fulfill a special calling.

For his Jewish adversaries, however, this divine choosing of Israel means that God is obliged to bless them, no matter what their spiritual state. As some have said, "All Israel has a share in the age to come." National Jewish identity is the primary and fundamental thing. This alone brings the blessing of God. Acceptance or rejection of Jesus as Messiah cannot alter this basic fact.

For St. Paul, on the other hand, if any Jew knowingly and finally rejects Jesus as Messiah and turns against Him, his sins will bring the wrath of God, and being a part of Israel will not save him. For Paul, faithfulness to God and His Christ is the primary and fundamental thing, and this reality and grace transcend all earthly categories, so that the Gentiles can be included too. Israel is indeed called by God to fulfill a special role, but this alone does not guarantee immunity from judgment.

In this section, the apostle writes to defend himself, for nothing he has written about the irrelevance of the Law means that he is anti-Jew or that he denies the special calling of Israel. He writes to explain in what the call of Israel truly consists and the significance of the inclusion of the Gentiles.

9 1 ***The*** **truth I speak in Christ! I do not lie—my conscience co-witnessing to me in *the* Holy Spirit,**
2 **that *there* is great sorrow and unceasing pain in my heart.**
3 **For I could pray *that* I myself were accursed from Christ on behalf of my brothers, my kinsmen according to the flesh,**
4 **who are Israelites, whose are the adoption-as-sons, and the glory and the covenants and giving-of-the-Law and the *Temple*-worship and the promises,**
5 **whose are the Fathers and from whom *is* the Christ, according to the flesh—God who is over all *be* blessed to the ages! Amen.**

St. Paul begins by calling God to witness his truthfulness as a Christian (the word **truth** stands at the head of the sentence in the original Greek, for greater emphasis) and insisting that he does **not lie.** Not only does he witness to the truth, but his **conscience**, formed and sensitive to the **Holy Spirit**, also **co-witnesses** to the truth of what he has to say. Such strong language is necessary because many of his Jewish detractors will find what he has to say incredible—namely that there is **great sorrow and unceasing pain** in his heart as he grieves for his Jewish countrymen. They think that he is their enemy and that he hates them. On the contrary, he passionately insists, he loves them and **could pray that** he himself **were accursed** and cut off **from Christ** if only this might save them. So far from delighting in their downfall, he would trade his salvation for theirs, his true **brothers** and **kinsmen**, if only it could be so.

He does not undervalue his ancestral heritage; he glories in it. How could he not love his kinsmen?—they are **Israelites**, heir to all the sacred history of salvation and the many divine gifts God has given to them alone. To them belongs **the adoption-as-sons**. God took Israel as His own, caring for them as a father cares for his own son (see Is. 64:8; Hos. 11:1–4), protecting them and teaching them. He dwelt among them in **the glory** of the Divine Presence, resting upon the Ark of their wilderness wandering and upon the Solomonic Temple (Ex. 40:34, 35; 1 Kings 8:10, 11), manifesting Himself openly in Israel as He had nowhere else.

To Israel belong **the covenants** and agreements that God made with Abraham, Isaac, and Jacob, promising to them and their seed that they would inherit the land, and with David and his seed, that He would establish their house forever (Gen. 17:1, 2; 2 Sam. 7:11–13). To Israel belongs **the giving-of-the-Law** (Gr. *nomothesia*; see Gr. *Nomos*, Law). This bestowal of the Law on Mount Sinai is the great gift of God to His People, given in power and fearful majesty, when God spoke to His People face to face (Ex. 19:16–20), entrusting them with a revelation of His character and will such as He had never given to any other nation (Ps. 147:20). At the heart of this Law are the prescriptions for **the *Temple*-worship** (Gr. *latreia*). These were given so that God could dwell among them in His holiness, a source of blessing to His people.

To Israel belong **the promises** given to the Patriarchs—promises of their glorious destiny in the land—promises that would culminate in Christ (Gal. 3:16f). To them belong **the Fathers** themselves, recipients of the promises and conduits of Israel's divine destiny, to whom they can look with pride as their noble ancestors.

Most importantly, from Israel came **according to the flesh** (that is, through historical descent) **the Christ** Himself, the goal and crown of all this salvation history. He is their great boast and their glory. Contemplating all these privileges and how they culminate in his blessed Lord Jesus, Paul breaks forth into a cry of praise, blessing **to the ages** the **God who is over all** and who orders the history of Israel and of all the world. (It is grammatically possible to take *God over all* as a further description of *the Christ*, but this would be contrary to St. Paul's normal usage, which reserves the term *God* for the Father—see 1 Cor. 15:24–28. Further, the apostle often bursts out with a blessing to God the Father, such as in 1:25; 2 Cor. 11:31.)

In rehearsing the privileges of Israel's sacred history, St. Paul places himself squarely in the midst of it, owning it as a loyal Jew. How could he ever hate his **kinsmen**, heirs to such good things? Their opposition to Christ does not make him hate them. On the contrary, he grieves over their fall, as over his true and beloved **brothers**.

6 But it is not as if the Word of God had fallen-down. For not all those from Israel *are* Israel,
7 neither are they all children because they are seed of Abraham, but "In Isaac your seed will be called."
8 That is, not the children of the flesh *are* the children of God, but the children of the promise are reckoned for seed.
9 For this *is* the word of promise: "According to this time, I will come and there will be to Sarah a son."
10 And not *this* only, but also Rebekah, having bed from one *man*, our father Isaac.
11 For though the *twins* were not yet born, nor practicing anything good or base, in order that God's purpose according to choice might remain, not out of works, but out of the One who calls,

> 12 **it was said to her, "The greater will serve** ***as slave*** **to the lesser."**
> 13 **Even as it is written, "Jacob I loved, but Esau I hated."**

Here the apostle takes up his argument and defense. His Jewish opponents argue that God promised to bless Israel, and if He does not do so—punishing them instead for their rejection of Jesus—then **the Word of God** promising to bless them has utterly **fallen-down** and failed.

This Paul utterly denies. God indeed promised to bless Israel. But who is Israel? In what does this company consist? His adversaries say, "Israel consists of every single Jew, every single person of Jewish national descent." For them, true Israel is defined entirely in national and racial terms. But for Paul, Israel was never defined that way, but in terms of God's choice and man's faithfulness. Thus, **not all those from** [racial] **Israel** ***are*** [true] **Israel**. That is, it is possible to be racially descended from Jacob and the Patriarchs and still not be part of God's People. Merely being racially the **seed of Abraham** does not automatically make the Jews his true spiritual **children** and heirs of God's blessing and covenant.

In confirmation of this, St. Paul calls attention to what God originally said to Abraham: **In Isaac your seed will be called**. That is, there was a principle of selection between sons even from the beginning, whereby one was chosen to be part of God's plan and people and one was not. God's word to Abraham to bless his children was based on a **word of promise**, such as was given to Sarah, when He promised, "**According to this time, I will come and there will be to Sarah a son**" (Gen. 18:10). That is, though Abraham had two sons—Isaac and Ishmael—one son, Isaac, was born according to God's promise, and the other son, Ishmael, was not. It was only the one born according to promise that was **reckoned** as Abraham's true spiritual **seed** and part of **the children of God**. Ishmael, though as much Abraham's son as Isaac, was nonetheless not reckoned as part of the covenant, because he was not born according to the promise.

And this was seen not only in the case of Abraham, but also more dramatically in the case of his son Isaac, for this principle of selection was not a one-time occurrence, but an ongoing principle. Thus, **our father Isaac** took **Rebekah** as his wife. This Rebekah had **bed** (Gr. *koiten*, used for a physical bed in Luke 11:7 and euphemistically for sexual relations in Rom. 13:13) from a single man, her husband, and had twins by him, the elder Esau and the younger Jacob. Even before the twins were born, when they had not yet **practiced anything** either **good or base** (and thus had no individual merit on which they could be judged), God still said, "**The greater will serve *as slave* to the lesser**" (Gen. 25:23). That is, God sovereignly chose **the lesser**, Jacob, to be heir of His messianic promises, and not **the greater** and older one, Esau. Jacob's descendants were to be included in the People of God, and Esau's descendants were to be made subject to them.

This was confirmed by the Prophet Malachi, through whom God said, "**Jacob I loved, but Esau I hated**" (Mal. 1:2f). Malachi was speaking, of course, not of God's personal distaste for Esau or of His personal delight in Jacob. As the context of Malachi's prophecy shows, he was referring to *the nations* descended from Jacob and Esau, namely the nations of Israel and Edom. Jacob was **loved** and chosen in that his descendants were made the recipients of messianic blessing; Esau was **hated** and rejected in that his descendants were judged for their sins and subjugated to Israel. This instance of the difference between Jacob and Esau is an even more dramatic illustration of the principle of divine choice, for Isaac and Ishmael, though of the same father, had different mothers, whereas Jacob and Esau had the same father and the same mother.

Thus, the example of Jacob and Esau clearly illustrates **God's purpose according to choice**. That is, it shows how God's principle of inclusion in His People Israel was **not out of works** (for a choice was made between Jacob and Esau before either had **practiced anything good or base**) but rather on the basis of **the One who calls**. God sovereignly chose one son and not the other on the basis of His own purposes and according to His own criteria, and not on the basis of racial descent alone. In the same way, St. Paul means to show, God in this day chooses who is to be truly a part of Israel on the basis of their inner faithfulness to Him and His Christ, and not simply on the basis of being racially Jewish. In this day as in days of old, what matters is the purpose of **the One who calls**—not the works or will of the one who desires to be called.

14 What therefore shall we say? *Is there* unrighteousness with God? May it never be!

15 For He says to Moses, "I will have mercy on whom I have mercy and I will have compassion on whom I have compassion."

16 So then *it is* not of the one willing nor the one running, but of the One having mercy—God.

17 For the Scripture says to Pharaoh, "For this very *thing* I raised you up, so that I may demonstrate in you My power and that My Name might be declared in all the earth."

18 So then He has mercy on whom He wills and He hardens whom He wills.

St. Paul then deals with an objection. "If that is the case," says the Jewish objector, "then there is **unrighteousness with God**." For according to this Jewish view, God is obliged to bless all the race of Israel, whether or not they accept Jesus as Messiah. Paul emphatically denies this, saying, **May it never be!** God is not obliged to bless anyone, but rather, as He said to Moses after Israel's apostasy with the golden calf, "**I will have mercy on whom I have mercy and I will have compassion on whom I have compassion**" (Ex. 33:19). That is, His favor always comes as undeserved grace. Israel can never deserve His mercy or compassion. He is never obliged to bless. His **mercy** and **compassion** never depend upon **the one willing** or desiring, nor on the one **running** and straining to earn it, but solely upon **God** who gives **mercy**. The Jews think that because Israel insistently petitions God in the Temple and has striven through the years to impress Him with Pharisaic legalism, God must now bless them even if they reject Jesus. But that is not the case. The Most High is no man's debtor, but gives mercy and compassion according to His own purposes.

This is seen clearly in the example of Pharaoh. **For the Scripture says to Pharaoh, "For this very thing I raised you up, so that I may demonstrate in you My power and that My Name might be declared in all the earth"** (Ex. 9:16). (We may note in passing how St. Paul uses the terms *God* and *the Scripture* interchangeably, since Scripture is the true Word of God.) In this instance, the apostle calls attention to the sovereignty of God's purpose. Pharaoh was given power by God over all the earth so that he could serve God's purposes. After Pharaoh proudly opposed God, God hardened his heart in judgment to **demonstrate** His **power** through the plagues and the final victory at the Red Sea. In the case of Pharaoh, what matters is solely the purpose and will of God. Just as He **had mercy** on Moses because **He willed**, so also He **hardened** Pharaoh because **He willed**. (We may note in passing that here there is no injustice or arbitrariness in God's will, for He willed to have mercy on Moses when Moses submitted to Him and willed to harden Pharaoh after he opposed Him.) Thus, God cannot be unrighteous to reject some of racial Israel if they reject His purpose in Christ, for God's will and purpose are sovereign. God is beholden to no man.

19 You will say to me therefore, "Why then does He still blame? For who withstands His purpose?"

20 Rather, O man, who are you, who answer back to God? Will the *thing* molded say to the molder, "Why did you make me thus?"

21 Or does not the potter have authority over the clay, to make from the same lump this vessel for honor and that for dishonor?

> 22 **But what if God, willing to demonstrate the wrath and to make His power known, bore with much patience vessels of wrath fitted for destruction,**
> 23 **so that He might make known the riches of His glory upon the vessels of mercy, which He pre-prepared for glory,**
> 24 ***including* us, whom He also called, not from among Jews only, but also from among Gentiles.**

St. Paul then deals with a further reply. "If that is the case," replies his Jewish opponent, **"Why then does He still blame? For who withstands His purpose?"** That is, if God will harden Israel as a judgment on their own stubbornness, so that they persist in their chosen rebellious way, why does He then blame them and punish them for this rebellion? For how could they withstand this hardening?

In understanding the apostle's answer, we must first be clear about the nature of God's hardening. It is not the case that God hardens innocent hearts, overriding free will, so that Israel has no choice whether or not to rebel and reject Jesus. This hardening is the same as other hardenings and judgments in the Old Testament, in that it comes as the long-delayed punishment of sins that were once freely chosen. The Jews of Paul's day have long rebelled against God's will, and now, in Christ, judgment has finally fallen upon their pride, hardening them in their rebellion.

Thus, God's hardening of hearts only comes in response to man's prior sin. To use Paul's example, God hardened Pharaoh's heart as a punishment on his sin—but only after Pharaoh rebelled against God with implacable impenitence. God hardened Pharaoh into the attitude he had already steadfastly chosen.

Or, to take another example, we read of the wicked sons of Eli the priest. They rebelled against God and refused to repent even when rebuked because, it is said, "the Lord desired to put them to death" (1 Sam. 2:25). That is, as a punishment for their previous stubbornness, God further hardened their hearts, so that they rejected their father's rebuke. God's patience with them had run out, and His judgment fell. The sins they had once chosen were finally to find them out.

This is the judgment and hardening that St. Paul envisions for the Jews who rebelliously reject Christ. They have always rebelled against God and His Law, choosing legalism over love, self-righteousness over mercy, pride over humility. God has long since been **willing to demonstrate** His **wrath** against them for their sins and **make His power known** in judgment. But He held back, waiting until Christ should come, enduring **with much patience** all that these **vessels of wrath** did. For in Christ, all hearts would be revealed for what they were. The humility of the humble and penitent would be manifested and rewarded, and the pride of the arrogant and impenitent would be judged. The humble sinners—the tax-collectors and prostitutes—would come to Jesus in repentance, and the proud Pharisees would reject Him. Christ was appointed therefore "for the fall and rise of many in Israel, that the thoughts from many hearts may be revealed" (Luke 2:34, 35). The ministry of Christ thus results in the final and definitive judgment on the **vessels of wrath** in Israel (the proud Pharisaic Jews who rejected Jesus). They are rejected, and **the riches of His glory** are made known **upon the vessels of mercy** (the humble Jews who accept Him).

We can see how indignant St. Paul is at the presumption of his Jewish opponent. For his opponent insists that God is obliged to bless Israel and dares not judge them for their sins through this dispensation of Christ. **O man**, the apostle thunders back, O puny man—**who are you, who answer back to God?** Who are you to say that God may not finally judge such rebellion, having patiently held off for long years? That would be like the ***thing*** **molded** (such as a pot) **saying to the molder** and artisan, "**Why did you make me thus?**" Such absurd presumption! Obviously, **the potter has authority over the clay** to make whatever he likes. If he makes **from the same lump** of clay **this vessel for honor** (forming it into, perhaps, a wine cup) and **that** vessel **for dishonor** (forming it, say, into a chamberpot)—what has the clay to say about it? It is entirely the choice of the potter what he makes! It is the same with God's work in Israel. If God chooses to reward the humble with **the riches of His glory**, bestowing pardon and sonship upon them when they accept Jesus, and if He chooses to judge the proud, rejecting them from His favor and pouring out His **wrath** when they reject Christ, that is His choice. He is the Potter, not they.

Finally we may note in St. Paul's reply how this dispensation and arrangement of mercy and judgment in Christ was planned from the ages and is cosmic in scope. The **vessels of wrath** who reject Christ and suffer **destruction** are said to be **fitted** for it. (The word here translated *fitted* is the same word used in Mark 1:19—Gr. *katartizo*—and there translated "mended." The thought is of something being prepared for its designated use.) That is, those who rebel against Christ prepare themselves for their final destruction by their persistence in sin. All through their lives in this age, they store up wrath for themselves. But the **vessels of mercy** who accept Christ are not said to be "restored" or fitted for their glorious destiny, but rather are **pre-prepared** for it (Gr. *proetoimazo*). That is, their destiny is not simply the result of their actions in this age. Rather, their glorious sonship was prepared for by God before the world began, as He planned such a glorious sonship for those who would accept Christ. And this sonship of those whom He **called** in Christ included **those not from among Jews only, but also from among Gentiles**. This dispensation and plan in Christ is cosmic in scope, embracing the humble of all the earth.

25 **As also in Hosea He says, "I will call *those who were* not My people, 'My people' and her who was not beloved 'beloved,'**
26 **and it will be that in the place where it was said to them, 'You *yourselves* are not My people,' there they will be called 'sons of a living God.'"**

27 **And Isaiah cries out on behalf of Israel,**
"Though the number of the sons of Israel be
as the sand of the sea, the remnant will be saved,
28 **for the Lord will do *His* Word upon the earth,**
consummating and cutting *it* short."
29 **And just as Isaiah foretold, "Except *the* Lord**
of Sabaoth had left behind to us a seed, we
would have become as Sodom and would have
been made like Gomorrah."

This truth is confirmed and proven by St. Paul with quotes from the Law. As God says in Hosea 2:23 and 1:10, God's plan involves the acceptance of those who were previously not accepted—which can include Gentiles as well. In the first and historical layer of meaning, God's prophecy through Hosea was directed towards Israel. It was Israel that was rejected by God so as to be no longer His People and no longer His Beloved, and it was Israel who was welcomed back. It was they who were rejected at the Babylonian exile and restored to the land to be redeemed as the **sons of a living God**. But the apostle underscores the nature of this redemption as *a bestowal of status upon those who had no status.* Israel was rejected at the Exile so as to have no status before God—even as the Gentiles of the world had no status before Him. Salvation is not just a reward for past fidelity: it is a reconciliation of the estranged, and, as such, can be given to Gentiles equally with Jews.

Thus, for Hosea, Israel's salvation was not a matter of rewarding Israel's faithfulness. Indeed, the prophet Isaiah testifies that Israel *had* no faithfulness to reward, for he **cries out** emphatically, **"Though the number of the sons of Israel be as the sand of the sea, the remnant will be saved, for the Lord will do *His* Word upon the earth, consummating and cutting *it* short"** (Is. 10:22, 23). That is, most in Israel were unfaithful to God, so that He was forced to execute His **Word** of judgment upon them thoroughly and quickly. Indeed, as Isaiah said again (1:9), **Except *the* Lord of Sabaoth had left behind to us a seed** and a posterity, they would have been utterly destroyed like **Sodom** and **Gomorrah**. Most of

Israel rebelled against God's purposes, with only a small minority, a remnant, remaining faithful. Salvation for such a people was indeed a matter of being reconciled from their estrangement.

30 What shall we say then? That Gentiles, not pursuing righteousness, seized upon righteousness, even the righteousness which is by faith,
31 but Israel, pursuing a Law of righteousness, did not reach that Law.
32 Why? Because they did not pursue it by faith, but as though it were by works. They stumbled over the Stone of stumbling,
33 just as it is written, "Behold, I set in Zion a Stone of stumbling and a stumbling-block Rock, and he who has faith in Him will not be put to shame."

What then was the final result? **That Gentiles, not pursuing righteousness, seized upon righteousness, even the righteousness which is by faith, but Israel, pursuing a Law of righteousness, did not reach that Law.** That is, the Gentiles, who never strove to please God by obedience to the Mosaic Law, **seized upon** and attained that divine acceptance. God generously accepted them because of their **faith** and commitment to Jesus. But Israel, even though they strove to **pursue a Law of righteousness** and win the divine favor through the Law, did not **reach** their goal or attain what the Law promised. Here is paradox and irony. The Gentiles did not chase after divine favor, but attained it, whereas the Jews chased after it, but did not reach it. **Why?** How could such a thing be? Because Israel did not **pursue** their goal properly. They pursued the Law's goal of achieving favor with God as if it were something to be legalistically earned. They did not serve God with humble **faith** in His forgiveness and love, but strove to fulfill the Law self-righteously **as though** the goal could be reached by **works**. They served God in their pride, thinking their works of circumcision and Sabbath-keeping obligated God to bless them.

That was why they rejected Christ when He came, **stumbling over the Stone of stumbling.** For Christ proclaimed that God's love could not be earned by works of self-righteous pride, but could only be received in penitent humility. Because they were proud, they rejected such words, and the Lord proved to be an obstacle to them, tripping them up and making them fall into judgment. This too is what the prophet had spoken: **"Behold, I set in Zion a Stone of stumbling and a stumbling-block Rock, and he who has faith in Him will not be put to shame"** (Is. 28:16; 8:14 LXX). Christ came to trip up the proud who trust in their own works. It is **he who has faith** who will finally **not be put to shame** on the Last Day.

So St. Paul brings this stage of his argument to a first conclusion. He has argued that God's Word to bless Israel has not fallen to the ground, for it is only the humble penitents who accept Christ who are the true Israel—a group of penitents that includes the Gentiles as well. This is God's choice and predestined plan—a plan for judgment on the proud in Israel as well as for mercy on the humble. It is consistent with all God's dealings throughout Israel's history, it is thoroughly just, and it was foretold by the Prophets. Thus Paul is not being disloyal to his ancestral people by insisting that salvation is only through Christ. This is what the Word of God (9:6) says.

10 1 **Brothers, the good-pleasure of my heart and the supplication to God on behalf of them *is* for salvation.**

2 **For I witness to them that they have a zeal of God, but not according to real-knowledge.**

3 **For being ignorant of the righteousness of God and seeking to make their own righteousness stand, they did not submit themselves to the**

righteousness of God.
4 **For Christ is the end of the Law for righteousness to everyone who has faith.**

St. Paul continues with his discussion on the role and fate of Israel. Israel, he has argued, has failed to arrive at the goal of the Law (9:31), which is righteousness and the favor of God. Why? Because they fundamentally misunderstand the nature of that righteousness and of their own Law.

This is a true grief to the apostle. He repeats what he said before, assuring his readers that **the good-pleasure** and longing of his inner **heart**—and that for which he continually offers **supplication to God**—is their final **salvation**. When he comes into a town and preaches in the synagogues (see Acts 18:4), his burning desire is that the Jews there might respond to the Gospel and accept Jesus as their Messiah. They are all aflame with **a zeal of God**, and St. Paul can **witness** and confirm that they are all fervent to serve Him. But it does them no good, for it is **not according to real-knowledge** or a true and deep appreciation for what God really wants.

They are in fact **ignorant of the righteousness of God**. They do not know how God in His mercy lavishes forgiveness on those who come to Him with humble faith in Christ. Instead of simply bowing before God's love, they **seek to make their own righteousness stand** and justify themselves, refusing to **submit themselves to the righteousness of God**. The Law is their boast before the world, and they have allowed this divine gift to make them proud. They have the Law of God and others do not. *They* are not like the rabble of the world, who have no knowledge of God (see John 7:49). They are Jews! They thus love to feel themselves superior to others, and are loath to take their place with tax-collectors and sinners as debtors to the mercy of God. They refuse to see that divine favor is a free gift to the penitent and are determined to use their Law as an instrument for self-justification.

Thus they fail to perceive that **Christ is the end** (Gr. *telos*) and goal of their Law, that **everyone who has faith** might receive God's **righteousness** and favor. They imagine that the Law is somehow an end in itself—that "man was made for the Sabbath"—and that they were made to find life and fulfillment in the Law forever. The Law, as the expression and preserver of their national and racial identity, was to be eternal and the whole focus of their relationship with God. They do not see how the Law's supremacy in Israel is temporal, not eternal, and how it is merely one stage in their pilgrimage, not their final goal. *Christ* is that final goal, and the Law was given to lead Israel to *Him*. It is through faith in Him that **righteousness** is bestowed on **everyone who has faith**—on the impious sinner as well as the pious devotee.

❧ ❧ ❧ ❧ ❧

5 For Moses writes of the righteousness *which is* by *the* Law, that the man having done these things will live in them.
6 But the righteousness which is by faith speaks thus: "Do not say in your heart, 'Who will ascend into the heaven?' (that is, to bring Christ down),
7 or 'Who will descend into the abyss?' (that is, to bring Christ up from the dead)."
8 But what does it say? "The Word is near you, in your mouth and in your heart"—that is, the Word of faith which we herald,
9 that if you confess with your mouth *the* Lord Jesus and have faith in your heart that God raised Him from the dead, you will be saved,
10 for with *the* heart one has faith to righteousness and with *the* mouth one confesses to salvation.
11 For the Scripture says, "Everyone having faith in Him will not be put to shame."
12 For there is no distinction between Jew and Greek, for the same *is* Lord of all, rich to all who call-upon Him,

13 **for "Everyone who calls-upon the Name of the Lord will be saved."**

This is in accord with what Moses himself wrote about attaining **righteousness** (Lev. 18:5). For in the Law, there are two kinds of righteousness and two aspects of one's walk with God.

There is the **righteousness *which is* by *the* Law**—that is, the favor which comes to a man **having done** the things that the Law demands. If a man practices those things, he will **live in them** and enjoy the blessings of this temporal life by them. Thus, for example, the Law commands the pious to tithe, and to offer to God the fruit of his labor. If a man fulfills this command, God will "bless him, in all the work of his hand which he does" (Deut. 14:28, 29). Blessing, prosperity, health, and security come as the result of obedience. If a man does these things, God will reward him. If he does not, God will not reward him.

Side by side with this temporal righteousness is the **righteousness which is by faith**. This is a man's basic relationship of love and loyalty to God—the commitment that keeps him coming back to God in penitence when he sins, and in thankfulness when he does well. Thus a man has faith in God, "loving the Lord his God with all his heart, with all his soul and with all his might" (Deut. 6:5), abiding within God's covenant; it is this underlying faith that brings the **righteousness** and basic favor wherein God accepts and loves him. It is this faith that forms the context for all his striving to do God's commands and be rewarded. Thus, **the righteousness which is out of the Law** is subordinated to and dependent upon **the righteousness which is out of faith**. Though God rewards a man with temporal blessings only when he succeeds in fulfilling His commands, He yet loves him because, regardless of his sins and shortcomings, he cleaves to Him in faith, remaining within the covenant.

It is this latter kind of righteousness and this latter aspect of one's walk with God that the apostle focuses upon as the object of his own ministry. He points out that this kind of righteousness does not leave one's salvation a matter of uncertainty. Unlike the striving of the Pharisaic Jews, which makes the enjoyment of salvation dependent upon achieving a perfect spiritual score, **the righteousness which is out of faith** leaves salvation within the reach of all.

It is as the Scriptures say: **"Do not say in your heart, 'Who will ascend to heaven?' or 'Who will descend into the abyss?' The Word is near you, in your mouth and in your heart."** The quotation is from Deuteronomy 30:12–14. In its original context, it is a statement of how close at hand is obedience to God. God's Word and covenant with Israel is "not too difficult for them, nor was it out of reach" (Deut. 30:11). God has revealed His Word to them and called them into covenant with Himself. All that remains is for them to respond with loyalty and obedience. They do not have to **ascend to heaven** to discover what He has commanded, nor "cross the sea" to fetch it (Deut. 30:13). His Word is before them, "very near to them, that they might observe it." They are therefore to "love the Lord their God" and not "worship other gods" (Deut. 30:14, 16, 17). This covenant is "very near them," and they can recite it by heart and know what God wants.

St. Paul applies this timeless principle to the current proclamation of **the Word of faith which** he **heralds**, for he is preaching the same basic message of obedient love to God as is found in the Law. Whereas Moses said that one did not need to **ascend to heaven** or to "cross" the deep of "the sea" to find the Word of the Law, Paul applies this to the Word of Christ. As the Law was accessible to Israel then, so Christ is accessible to the believer now. One does not need to **ascend to heaven** in order to **bring Christ down** from there, nor **descend into the abyss** of the underworld **to bring Christ up from the dead**. Rather, Christ has come down from heaven to earth, has risen from the dead, and is even now accessible to the believer by faith. Thus, **the Word** of faith in Him is **near** the believer, **in his mouth and in his heart**, even as the Scripture says. Just as the covenant of faith in God was within the reach of every Jew, so saving faith in Christ is now within the reach of every Christian, whether Jew or Gentile. The Jew of old could recite with his lips what God had put in his heart and be in covenant with God. The Christian now can **confess with** his **mouth *the* Lord Jesus and have faith in** his **heart that God raised Him from the dead** and so **be saved**. As the Scripture says, being in the saving covenant with God is within easy reach. It is as easy as a simple confession of Christ made at baptism, springing from internal faith in Him. Moses of old spoke of the mouth and the heart. For Paul, this was a prophetic indication of the way of salvation in Christ, for **with *the* heart one has faith to righteousness and with *the* mouth one confesses to salvation.**

It is as another Scripture says, "**Everyone having faith in Him will not be put to shame**" (Isaiah 28:16). That is, vindication from God comes through simply coming to God in penitent faith—not with reliance upon former works. This is the faith confessed in baptism, as the candidate calls upon the Name of the Lord and has his sins washed away (Acts 22:16). For Paul, it is because this saving heart faith is confessed with the mouth in the baptismal waters that Moses was led to speak of the Word being "in the mouth and in the heart" (Deut. 30:14).

In this baptismal salvation, **there is no distinction between Jew and Greek**. God has so ordered the way of salvation that one is saved simply by having faith in the resurrected Christ and by confessing allegiance to Him. This way is open to all—Gentile as well as Jew. That is only fitting, since there is but One God—not one God for the Jews and another for the Gentiles. There is but One and the **same Lord of all**, He who is **rich to all who call-upon Him**—regardless of their race. That is, God wills to pour out His lavish grace upon *any* who will **call-upon** and invoke His mercy (Gr. *epikaleo*—meaning "to call down aid and rescue"). The one calling-upon Him does not have to be Jewish. This is what was foretold by the Prophet Joel: "**Everyone who calls-upon the Name of the Lord will be saved**" (Joel 2:32)—be he Jew or Gentile. In the messianic salvation, God's grace is poured out upon all.

14 How then shall they call-upon *Him* in whom they have not had faith? And how shall they have faith *in Him* whom they have not heard?

And how shall they hear without one heralding?
15 **And how shall they herald unless they are sent? Just as it is written, "How beautiful *are* the feet of those who preach the Gospel of good things!"**
16 **But they did not all obey the Gospel, for Isaiah says, "Lord, who had faith in *what was* heard *from* us?"**
17 **So faith comes from hearing and hearing through *the* Word of Christ.**

That the grace of God is thus available even to the Gentiles, then, legitimizes Paul's controversial mission. The Gentiles, equally with the Jews, can be saved if they **call-upon** the Lord in baptism. But how can the Gentiles invoke Him **in whom they have not had faith**? For the Gentiles have no prior knowledge of the God of Israel. For them to invoke Him, they must first be brought to faith. **And how shall they have faith *in Him* whom they have not heard?** If they are to believe in the God of Israel and His Messiah, they must first hear the Good News about what He has done. And how shall they hear that **without one heralding** that Good News as God's messenger? And how shall those messengers reach the Gentiles with that message **unless they are sent** as His apostles? (The word for *sent* is the Gr. *apostelo*, cognate with the word *apostolos*, "apostle.") That is why, St. Paul says, Isaiah wrote of the apostolic mission to the Gentiles, blessing the very **feet** of the ones who traveled from afar, **preaching the Gospel of good things**—for the word in the Greek of Isaiah 52:7 cited here is *euaggelizo*, cognate with the word *euaggelion*, "Gospel."

The fact, then, that all the Gentiles do not yet **obey the Gospel** is only to be expected, since all have not yet heard. This, the apostle says, can also be concluded from the words of Isaiah the Prophet (Is. 53:1), where he says, "**Lord, who had faith in *what was* heard *from* us?**" (Gr. *Tis episteusen te akoe emon?*) That is, Isaiah speaks of having **faith** (Gr. *pistis*) as the result of **hearing** (Gr. *akoe*). From this the apostle concludes that **faith comes from hearing** the message, and this possibility of **hearing** only comes through the apostolic preaching of the **Word of Christ**.

Thus, this divine salvation given to the true Israel and received by faith alone (9:6; 10:9) must be offered to the Gentiles too. Paul's controversial mission, seen by so many of his Jewish countrymen as a repudiation of his Jewish heritage, is nothing else than the fulfillment of the ancient prophecies to Israel.

18 But I say, surely they did not hear? Indeed *they did*: "Into all the earth their sound went out and to the ends of the world their words."

Here the apostle begins to deal with another series of objections from his Jewish opponent. **But surely**, his opponent replies, the Gentiles **did not hear**, did they? God *never* spoke to the nations, but was always concerned only for Israel. On the contrary, replies the apostle, **indeed** the Gentiles *did* hear from God and received His Word. It is as the Psalmist said, "**Into all the earth** did the **sound** of God's messages go out, and these **words** went out even **to the ends of the world**" (Ps. 19:4). The Psalmist is referring to the revelation of God's glory, which He revealed to all the world through the splendor of His creation. "The heavens told the glory of God," declaring that they were "the work of His hands"—a silent message to all the earth of the power of Israel's God, and a testimony of His universal care. He did not abandon the world when He spoke His special Word of revelation to Israel, but spoke to the Gentiles also, "revealing knowledge" through the starry expanse of heaven (Ps. 19:1, 2). Paul's opponents thus cannot say that God always cared only for Israel.

19 But I say, surely Israel did not know? First Moses says, "I will provoke you to jealousy by

> **that which is not a nation, by an uninsightful**
> **nation will I anger you."**
> **20 But Isaiah is very daring and says, "I was found**
> **by those who did not seek Me; I became mani-**
> **fest to those who did not ask for Me."**
> **21 But to Israel He says, "All the day, I reached**
> **My hands towards a disobedient and contra-**
> **dicting people."**

But Paul's opponents bring forth another objection. **But surely, Israel did not know** of such care for the Gentiles, did they? How could they be expected to accept such novelties? On the contrary, says St. Paul, from the very **first**, way back at the time of **Moses**, the great Lawgiver himself prophesied, "**I will provoke you to jealousy by that which is not a nation, by an uninsightful nation will I anger you**" (Deut. 32:21). This is from the Song of Moses, which he taught Israel as an abiding cultural reminder of their national tendency to apostasy and the consequent need for repentant trust in Yahweh. For he "knew that after his death" Israel would "act corruptly and turn away from the way which he had commanded" them, so he "spoke in their hearing the words of this song" as a corrective (Deut. 31:29, 30). **That which is not a nation**—a people so contemptible as to be scarcely reckoned a proper nation at all—an **uninsightful nation** which worships dead idols—these were the chosen vessels of God to **provoke** Israel. In its original context, it meant that God would use these Gentiles to punish Israel, provoking them by invasion and subjugation, causing them to cry out to Yahweh for rescue, making them jealous of the pagan victories. In Paul's day, God is using the Gentiles to provoke Israel by granting His mercy to those **uninsightful** and formerly benighted pagans, making Israel jealous of the Gentiles' privileges. In both cases, the divine strategy is the same: to grant something to the Gentiles that He has not given to Israel. Paul's Jewish opponent cannot say that Israel could not have known about God's care for the nations.

In fact, the apostle continues, the Scriptures are even *more* clear about God's mercy on the Gentiles. Not only did Moses declare this principle at the very **first**, but later on **Isaiah** was even more bold and **very daring**, speaking the truth plainly. While God **was found** by those Gentiles who formerly **did not seek** Him, Israel actively turned away from Him! "**All the day**, God **reached** His **hands towards** Israel, but they remained **a disobedient and contradicting people**" (Is. 65:1, 2 LXX). Given such frankness of speech, Israel has no excuse not to know such things!

11 1 I say then, has God pushed-aside His People? May it never be! For I *myself* am also an Israelite, of *the* seed of Abraham, of *the* tribe of Benjamin!

2 God has not pushed-aside His People whom He foreknew. Or do you not know what the Scripture says in *the part about* Elijah, how he appeals to God against Israel?

3 "Lord, they have killed Your prophets, they have razed Your altars, and I alone am left, and they are seeking my soul."

4 But what says the *divine*-pronouncement to him? "I have left for Myself seven thousand men who have not bent *the* knee to Baal."

5 Thus then, there has also come to be at the present *appointed*-time a remnant according to the choice of grace.

6 (But if *it is* by grace, it is no longer out of works, otherwise grace is no longer grace.)

7 What then? What Israel is seeking-after, this it has not attained, but the chosen attained it, and the rest were hardened,

8 just as it is written, "God gave them a spirit of deep-sleep, eyes to see not and ears to hear not,

down to this very day."
9 **And David says, "Let their table become a snare**
and a trap, and a stumbling-block and a rec-
ompense to them.
10 **"Let their eyes be darkened to see not and bend**
their back through all *time*."

The apostle then deals with another Jewish objection. **I say then,** says the objector, does this not mean that **God has pushed-aside** and repudiated **His People**? For Paul has said that Israel did not arrive at the goal of righteousness that they were pursuing (9:31). What else can this mean but that God has rejected the very People He once promised to bless?

St. Paul rejects this conclusion, saying **May it never be!** God would never push-aside the People He **foreknew** and chose from all eternity! Paul himself is evidence of that! He himself (the Gr. *ego* is emphatic) is such an **Israelite, of *the* seed of Abraham, of *the* tribe of Benjamin**. That is, he himself is heir to the whole history of salvation promises given to Abraham and all his descendants after him. That he enjoys the divine favor shows that God is still with His covenant People.

Or has his opponent never read his own Scriptures? For **in *the part about*** **Elijah** (1 Kings 19), Elijah feared that God's covenant people no longer existed. Elijah had been ruthlessly persecuted by King Ahab and his wife Jezebel. They had **killed** God's **prophets** and **razed** His **altars** so that Elijah feared that he **alone** was **left**—and they were **seeking** his **soul**, to kill him too! All of Israel had become apostate, following Ahab in worshipping Baal. Elijah alone was the last true Jew! What did the ***divine*-pronouncement** say to him? **"I have left for Myself seven thousand men who have not bent *the* knee to Baal"** (1 Kings 19:18). That is, God's *true* Israel—the authentic Jews in whom His covenant blessings were to be realized—was the faithful **remnant**, the **seven thousand who had not bent the knee to Baal**. Those who worshipped Baal were apostate and not the true Israel. God had promised to abide with His People, and this promise was fulfilled in this remnant. This was always His way. The Jews who rebelled against God through the ages were never reckoned as part of His true People, but only the pious faithful were. They and they alone were to be the recipients and beneficiaries of God's covenant of blessing.

In Paul's day also, **the present *appointed*-time** and day of opportunity (Gr. *kairos*), this remnant exists also. It is **according to the choice of grace**—that is, according to God's gracious choosing. God chooses those who respond to His grace in Christ as His faithful remnant and His true People. (But this means, St. Paul adds, that Jewish **works** are by definition excluded, for **otherwise grace is no longer grace**. That is, God does not choose those Jews who fulfill the **works** of circumcision and Sabbath, but those who simply respond to His **grace** and pardon. That is, after all, what *grace* means.)

What then is the final result? That **what Israel is seeking-after** is the very thing it **has not attained**. Rather, **the chosen attained it, and the rest were hardened**. That is, only those Jews whom God chooses in Christ on the basis of their coming to Him penitently in faith are reckoned as the true remnant. **The rest**, those who rejected Christ, **were hardened** as a judgment on their sins and their pride.

This is exactly what was prophesied in the Scriptures. As Isaiah foretold of such, "**God gave them a spirit of deep-sleep, eyes to see not and ears to hear not**" (Is. 29:10). That is, those who opposed God's purposes were rendered incapable of spiritual insight. And this is not simply what God did once; it is His habitual way of dealing with rebels **down to this very day**. Indeed, as David himself said, the very works and prosperity and blessings they enjoyed were to work against them. Their sacrificial altar-**table**—their own religious works—were to **become a snare and a trap, and a stumbling-block and a recompense to them** (Ps. 69:22, 23 LXX). Trusting in their sacrifices, they fell into the snare of God's judgment. This blindness and judgment were definitive and final. It was not a temporary punitive measure that would pass. If they rejected Christ, there was no hope. God's wrath would **bend their back through all *time*.**

EXCURSUS:

On the Church as Israel

For St. Paul, the true Israel is the faithful Israel—those Jews who are faithful to God and who, as such, believe in His Messiah. The Jewish nation is therefore divided into those Jews who reject Jesus (and who are therefore not the true Israel, but apostate, even as the Jews who worshipped Baal in the days of Elijah were apostate) and those Jews who accept Jesus as Messiah (and who are therefore the faithful remnant and the true Israel, chosen by God according to His grace).

It is in this Jewish remnant that the promises of God to Israel are fulfilled, and it is this remnant that is thus the true "commonwealth of Israel" (Eph. 2:12) and the true "Israel of God" (Gal. 6:16). Thus St. Paul can declare to his fellow Jews that he is suffering imprisonment for the Gospel "for the sake of the hope of Israel" (Acts 28:20), for the Christian movement is nothing else than the embodiment of all the aspirations of Israel and the carrier of its divine destiny.

This Jewish remnant soon came to be joined by many Gentiles—especially through the apostleship and labors of St. Paul. The addition of these Gentiles, however, does not make the Christian Church any less Jewish nor any less the remnant and true Israel. Regardless of the number of Gentiles—whether there are but a few Gentiles sprinkled among the Jewish majority (as in the early days of the Church) or whether the Gentiles outnumber the Jews (as in later years)—the Church maintains its identity as the commonwealth of Israel and the historic People of God.

The Church therefore is the true Israel, *not* in the sense that the Gentiles have *supplanted* the Jews, taking from them their status as the People of God, but in the sense that many faithful Gentiles have *joined* faithful Jews in their worship of Messiah, and have partaken *with* them of their covenant status as the true Israel. Those Jews who accept Jesus as Messiah (together with their Gentile brothers) still form the true Israel. Those Jews who reject their Messiah, though still "beloved" by God and called to salvation, are not true Israel, but have, by their unbelief, forfeited their claim to be the People of God.

11 I say then, did they trip so as to fall? May it never be! But by their offense salvation *has come* to the Gentiles, to provoke them to jealousy.
12 Now if their offense *means* riches of the world and their defeat *means* riches of the Gentiles, how much more will their fullness *mean*!
13 But I speak to you who are Gentiles. Inasmuch then as I *myself* am an apostle of *the* Gentiles, I glorify my service,
14 if somehow I might provoke to jealousy those of my flesh and save some of them.
15 For if their loss *means* the reconciliation of *the* world, what will *their* acceptance *mean*, if not life from the dead?
16 Now if the first-fruit *is* holy, *then* also the lump, and if the root *is* holy, *so* also the branches.

The apostle deals with one final Jewish objection. "If what Paul says is true," the objector says, "then Israel **tripped so as to fall**—Israel as a whole is entirely irrelevant to the purposes of God. Israel is entirely ruined and God can have no further use for them!"

Once again, St. Paul denies this, with his customary **May it never be!** Israel still has its place in the divine plan. For **by their offense salvation has come to the Gentiles**.

Here the apostle steps back to survey the global situation regarding Israel and the Gentile nations. Formerly, Israel kept its faith in the one true God completely to itself. They may have been called to be lights to those in darkness and teachers of the world (see 2:19), but as a whole, they retreated to within the safe and sacred borders of their own chosenness. They preferred to treat their faith as a privilege to be guarded rather than as a treasure to be shared, leaving the Gentiles in the same heathen darkness of idolatry in which they found them. But, after Israel as a whole had rejected Christ, the offer of the Gospel was taken with greater fervor to the Gentiles (see Acts 13:45, 46) and these Gentiles accepted the Gospel with great openness. Thus, the **offense** of the nation of Israel and their spiritual **defeat** in rejecting Christ meant **riches** for **the world** of **the Gentiles**. Thus, Israel still has a pivotal role—even in unbelief!

This inclusion of the Gentiles also is to have a saving effect on Israel. They are to see such privileges and joy given to their former Gentile foes and be **provoked to jealousy**. Here are these benighted Gentiles delighting in *their* Scriptures, worshipping *their* Messiah, loving *their* ancestral God, and overflowing with joy! How can they let the pagans alone have all this? This, St. Paul confides to those **who are Gentiles**, is really why he **glorifies** his **service** and ministry (Gr. *diakonia*) and so zealously works to reach the Gentiles. It is not, he says, just for you Gentiles alone! Rather, he always has a backward glance at his beloved countrymen of his **flesh**, that he might also **save some of them**. The conversion of Israel remains in the apostle's heart as his final joy and ultimate goal.

For, if Israel is so fruitful in their unbelief and exclusion from the Kingdom that **their loss** ***means*** **the reconciliation of** ***the*** Gentile **world, how much more** will Israel bear fruit in their **fullness**, when they are included in the Kingdom through their repentant faith! If Israel's unbelief means the nations' reconciliation, surely their believing would mean **life from the dead**! When all Israel shall come to faith, surely it will herald the Second Coming and the final resurrection!

Israel, then, retains its place in the divine plan of God for the salvation of the world. It remains **holy** and dedicated to the purposes of God. For **if the first-fruit** of grain is holy, then so is the whole **lump** of dough made from it (see Num. 15:17–20); and **if the root** of a plant is holy, then obviously **the branches** drawing life from that root are holy too. It is the same with Israel. The Patriarchs are **the first-fruits** and **the root** of the nation. These men were **holy** in that they had their share in the cosmic saving purposes of God. This being so, then obviously the nation derived from them is **holy** too and inherits this place in the divine dispensation.

17 But if some of the branches were broken-off and you, a wild-olive, were grafted-in among them and became a fellow-communicant of the root of the fatness of the olive tree,
18 do not boast-off *against* the branches, but if you do boast-off, remember that you do not bear the root, but the root *bears* you.
19 You will say then, "Branches were broken-off that I *myself* might be grafted-in."
20 *You say* aright. For their faithlessness they were broken-off, but you stand by faith. Do not mind high *things*, but fear,
21 for if God did not spare the branches according to nature, neither will He spare you.
22 Behold then the kindness and the severity of God! To those who fell, severity, but to you, the kindness of God, if you abide on in kindness, since *otherwise* you also will be cut-off.
23 And they also, if they do not abide on in faithlessness, will be grafted-in, for God is able to graft them in again.
24 For if you were cut-off from what is according to nature a wild-olive and were against nature grafted-in into a cultivated-olive-tree, how

much more will these who are according to nature be grafted-in to their own olive-tree?

St. Paul now turns from answering Jewish objections to rebuking possible Gentile arrogance. In the divine plan, God used the loss and rejection of the nation of Israel to bring blessing to the Gentiles. Given the mutual hostility that historically characterized Jewish-Gentile relations, it is possible that some Gentiles in Rome might use this truth to exult over the Jews and **mind high *things*,** setting their mind on their own supposed superiority. They might be tempted to **boast-off** (Gr. *katakauxaomai*—meaning not just "to boast" [Gr. *kauxaomai*]—but "to boast *against*, to crow, to 'mouth off'"). This was unacceptable behavior and, given Israel's history, completely inappropriate.

Building on the analogy of the Jews of that day being the **branches** growing from the **root** of the Patriarchs (v. 16), the apostle admits that **branches** (the Jews) **were broken-off** in order that the Gentiles **might be grafted-in** in their place. But these Gentile branches should remember they are not native-grown olive branches that naturally grew from an olive root, but are **wild-olive** branches, grafted-in to become **fellow-communicants** and sharers of **the root of the fatness of the olive tree**. That is, they partake of the rich root of the olive tree, to which they are not naturally entitled and which is naturally foreign to them. As wild-olive branches, they should be grateful to share the rich life of the olive tree—and not the poor life natural to wild-olive trees. Thus, they should **remember** that it is not they who **bear** and carry the **root**, but rather **the root** that **bears** them. The root of Jewish heritage is not somehow dependent upon the Gentile Christians. Rather, they are the dependent beneficiaries of Israel—and should therefore not **boast-off** against the Jews, but show some gratitude and respect to them. They were not rejected by God because their Jewishness was to be despised (as the Gentiles may easily have imagined). They are rejected by Him solely **for their faithlessness** and unbelief in Jesus—just as the Gentiles themselves **stand** firm in God's favor only **by faith**. Instead of showing a superior and racist attitude toward the Jews and presumption towards

God, they should more appropriately walk in godly **fear** and humility. For **if God did not spare** the natural branches of the Jews, but cut off branches natural to the Jewish root, how much less likely is He to **spare** them (who are not natural to that root) if they fall away from faith?

From this they can appreciate both **the kindness and the severity of God**—to the Jews **who fell, severity**, in casting them out of His favor; to those Gentiles who trust in Jesus, **the kindness of God** Himself—but only if they **abide on** in that kindness. If pride and presumption cause them to fall away, they too will be **cut-off** even as Israel was. All that matters is faithfulness to God.

In fact, if these faithless Jews renounce their **faithlessness** and unbelief and return to faith, they will be quickly **grafted in again**! God **is able** and more than willing to do this. For if the Gentiles were **against nature grafted-in into a cultivated-olive-tree**, sharing a Jewish inheritance to which they have no historical right, **how much more** will the Jews be **grafted-in to their own olive-tree**, sharing the salvation which is theirs **according to nature** and historical right? Let the Gentiles remember all this and walk in humility, not in anti-Semitic conceit!

25 For I do not want you to be ignorant, brothers, of this mystery, lest you be prudent in your own *eyes*, that hardness in part has happened to Israel until the fullness of the Gentiles has come in,
26 and thus all Israel will be saved, just as it is written, "The Rescuer will come out of Zion; He will turn away impiety from Jacob,
27 and this *is* the covenant from Me when I take away their sins."
28 According to the Gospel *they are* enemies because of you, but according to the choice *they are* beloved because of the Fathers,

29 for the *spiritual*-gifts and the calling of God *are* unregretted.

The apostle comes to the final part of his discussion on the role of Israel. He is determined that the Gentile Romans know this **mystery** or new revelation given to initiated Christians, because he wants to preserve them in humility and does not want them to consider themselves to be **prudent**, or sophisticated and wise in their **own** *eyes*. They should be informed that **hardness in part has happened to Israel until the fullness of the Gentiles has come in, and thus all Israel will be saved**. That is, the way in which Israel will finally reach salvation is **thus** (Gr. *outos*, "in this manner")—by enduring a partial hardening **until** such a time as **the fullness of the Gentiles** should come to faith. When the **fullness** of the nations shall at length **come in**, then the providential hardening will have accomplished its purpose and will be ended. Israel's apostasy is therefore not permanent, nor does it mean that God has abandoned His ancient covenant. Rather, their judgment and apostasy are a part of God's larger plan for the redemption of the world and, when it has fulfilled its purpose for the nations, it will end. That is how Israel will be saved: by God using their unbelief to bring in the nations.

This was foretold by the Prophets as well. As Isaiah said, "**The Rescuer will come out of Zion; He will turn away impiety** and apostasy **from Jacob**"; and this is how **the covenant** from God will be manifested (Is. 59:20, 21). To this citation, St. Paul adds a line as well from Isaiah 27:9 (LXX), to stress that this divine covenant consists of God **taking away their sins**. (St. Paul also says that the Rescuer will come *out of* Zion—and not "*to* Zion," as the Hebrew text says, or "*on behalf of* Zion," as the Greek LXX says. Probably this change is an echo of Ps. 14:7—which speaks of "the salvation of Israel" coming "*out of* Zion"—and was made in order to stress how this salvation of Israel restores and ends their long "captivity.") By these references, the apostle means to show how the Scriptures themselves foretold this hardening and apostasy in Israel. God's faithfulness to His **covenant** consisted in overcoming their **impiety** and unbelief—not in rewarding their righteousness.

Thus, Israel should not be despised or dismissed. True, **according to the Gospel** standpoint, ***they are*** **enemies** of God. Because of their rejection of Christ, they have forfeited divine favor and salvation. Yet **according to the choice** of God, when He entered into covenant with the Patriarchs, in a sense they are still **beloved because of** those **Fathers**, and still have a place in God's final plan. That is because the ***spiritual*****-gifts** (Gr. *charismata*) of God's freely given covenants and God's **calling** to be His People are **unregretted** by Him and forever in force. (The Greek word translated *unregretted—ametameleta*—is the same word used in 2 Cor. 7:10 to describe the unregretted repentance of the believer, which leads to life.) Thus, God does not regret calling Israel to be His People, and He strives with them that they should fulfill that calling by coming to Christ.

---

30 For just as you *yourselves* were once disobedient to God but now have received mercy because of their disobedience,
31 thus these also now have been disobedient, that through the mercy shown to you, they also may now receive mercy.
32 For God has enclosed all in disobedience that He might show mercy to all.

The apostle sums up the role of Israel in the plan of God, declaring again how God's glorious plan for the ages was to **show mercy to all** who were **enclosed in disobedience**. Through His providence, God allowed all men to go their own way, **enclosing** them and leaving them in the prison of their own **disobedience**, that they might experience the depth of their plight and cry out to Him for help. Thus their own apostasy will teach them how bitter it is to forsake their God (Jer. 2:19).

All are left to their disobedience: they themselves, the Gentiles, **were once disobedient to God** as idolatrous pagans. The Jews have

now been disobedient in their rejection of Christ. The disobedient Gentiles **now have received mercy** and received the Gospel because of Jewish **disobedience**. And the unbelieving Jews, when they see **the mercy shown to** the Christian Gentiles, will themselves repent and **receive mercy** too. God's aim is to show mercy on the whole disobedient world, using the works of one group to reach the other. Man's sin cannot deflect God from His purposes of universal mercy—whether man is obedient or disobedient, God will work through either to bring all to salvation.

33 Oh, *the* depth of riches and wisdom and knowl-
edge of God! How unsearchable His judg-
ments, and untraceable His ways!
34 For "who has known the mind of the Lord, or
who has become His counselor?"
35 Or "who pre-gave to Him and it will be rec-
ompensed to him?"
36 For from Him and through Him and to Him
***are* all things. To Him *be* glory to the ages.**
Amen.

So it is that St. Paul bursts into a heartfelt exclamation of praise, declaring the **depth** of God's **riches**, seen in both His **wisdom** and His **knowledge**. Both in the way God arranges the hidden patterns of history and in His working within the human heart, the fathomless riches of God's grace are seen. Who could have guessed how He would use Israel—calling them to salvation and choosing as His true remnant those who came to Christ, judging Israel by hardening them for their longstanding stubbornness and then using that unbelief to reach the rest of the world? Who could have foreseen such wonders? **How unsearchable** are these **judgments** and dealings with the children of men! It is as the Scripture itself says, "**Who has known the mind of the Lord?" Or "who pre-gave to Him**" that it might be "**recompensed to him**"? (Is. 40:13; Job 41:11). No one has been so wise as to function as God's advisor or been His benefactor so as to put Him in his debt! In all these mighty judgments and mighty deeds of salvation, God has acted sovereignly—unforeseen by men, the gracious Savior of all. Like a good Jew, St. Paul concludes with a doxology to the Father, the source, agent, and goal of all: **from Him and through Him and to Him *are* all things. To Him *be* glory to the ages. Amen.**

EXCURSUS:

On the Final Salvation of the Jews

In 11:25–27, St. Paul states that the salvation of all Israel will be accomplished only through their partial hardening, allowed as a punishment for their sins and to bring the Gospel to the Gentile world, so that **the fullness of the Gentiles** can come in. After that is accomplished, the need for that hardening will be ended and Israel will be saved.

When and how will this be? No one may know for certain, of course. As Origen said, what all this means "or what the fullness of the Gentiles will be, only God knows, along with His only-begotten Son and perhaps a few of His friends." Nonetheless, the following thoughts are offered.

The Gospel in the time of Paul was accepted by only a few Gentiles, though the Church nurtured the prophetic hope that one day all nations would come to Christ (see Is. 60:3). Since St. Paul's day, many nations have indeed come to the Lord and countless Gentiles have been saved. The phrase *the fullness of the Gentiles* (11:25) perhaps means all those Gentiles who will ever come to the Lord—the full complement of the saved from among all the nations throughout this age. During the final time of the End, when the Gospel will be preached in times of apocalyptic persecution, the choice between Christ and Satan, between Light and darkness, will be clear to all the world. During the days of the Antichrist, the issue will be plain. Those who are open to the light will all come to the faith and those who do not love the truth will flee from the Gospel and accept the lies of the Antichrist (2 Thess. 2). Those from the nations who then **come in** will represent the final **fullness of the Gentiles.**

It may be that the clarity of the eternal issues during those apocalyptic days and the purity of the Church under persecution will commend the Gospel to the Jews as it has not been effectively commended before. During these present times of relative peace, the sins of the Church make it hard for the Jews to recognize the Church as the true People of God, or be **provoked to jealousy** when they observe its life. Then, at the time of the End, the fire of persecution will purge away the Church's sins, allowing her true purity and life to shine through. Then, perhaps, the Jews may see as they never have before, and join in serving their Messiah. Then Israel's hardening will be over, their **impiety** removed and their **sins** taken away. The Jews will then fulfill God's unregretted calling to them to be the true People of God.

Notes for Section III:

ꕥ IV ꕥ

LIVING THE NEW LIFE IN CHRIST (12:1—13:14)

Given the change of tone and subject, it would seem as if St. Paul took a break from his dictation at the end of chapter 11 and returned later to resume writing chapter 12. This is in accordance with other of his Epistles, in which he first deals with doctrinal matters (e.g. Col. 1; 2) and then follows this up with practical exhortations (e.g. Col. 3; 4). Having explained to the Romans the Gospel he will preach when in Rome (chapters 1—8) and having added an explanatory excursus on the role of Israel (chapters 9—11), the apostle now offers a series of practical exhortations.

Like many Gentiles, the Christians of Rome entered the Church with many secular presuppositions and approaches. The world exercised a powerful influence on them, trying to squeeze them into its mold. Moreover, in their life as a Christian community, they may well have viewed their neighbors from a worldly perspective, standing independent and aloof from them, perhaps disdaining some and being in competition with others. As well, they may have had an attitude of hostility to the secular authorities, despising them for their secularity as if they were the enemies of God. And of course, like all pagans, they may not have appreciated the need for sexual restraint. St. Paul has therefore to exhort them to a new way of living. They are to reckon themselves dead to sin (6:11)—but what exactly does this entail in daily life?

§IV.1 Living as a holy sacrifice

12 1 **I exhort you, therefore, brothers, by the compassions of God, to present your bodies a living and holy sacrifice, well-pleasing to God, *which is* your rational worship.**
2 **And do not be conformed to this age, but be transfigured by the renewing of your mind, that you may prove what *is* the will of God, that which is good and well-pleasing and perfect.**

St. Paul bases his exhortation to live the new life in Christ on an appeal to **the compassions of God**, of which he has previously spoken. In the previous chapters he dwelt at length upon "the depth of the riches" of the "wisdom and knowledge of God" (11:33). **Therefore**, because of this great mercy offered to us, we must respond by **presenting** our **bodies** as a **living and holy sacrifice**, one which is **well-pleasing** and acceptable to Him. This is our true and **rational worship**.

The apostle is addressing the Roman Christians as a corporate body, and this sacrificial presentation is also a corporate one. It is, in fact, a reference to the weekly Eucharist. It is in the Eucharist that this sacrifice is made.

The Eucharist is our corporate and liturgical offering of the one, unique, and unrepeatable Sacrifice of Christ. On the Cross, He offered Himself as the Lamb of God, taking away the sins of the world, and He remained in heaven as the Lamb slain (Rev. 5:6), His Presence at God's right hand being our living and effectual intercession before the Father's throne (Heb. 7:25). In the Eucharist, the Church presents afresh that Sacrifice, making an *anamnesis* (or memorial) of it and knowing its presence and power in our midst. The Eucharist *is* therefore that Sacrifice, eternal in the heavens, present here in time on our altars.

But the Eucharist is not merely our offering and thankful presentation of Christ's Sacrifice. It is also, in union with that Sacrifice, the sacrifice of ourselves. For the Church that presents the sacrificial Body of Christ is also itself that Body. In the words of St. Augustine, "If you are the Body of Christ and His members, your mystery is presented at the Table of the Lord" (Sermon 272). In the Eucharist, Christ gathers us together with Himself, so that "we, who are many, are one Body, for we all partake of the one Bread" (1 Cor. 10:17). The Eucharist therefore constitutes the Church as Christ's Body.

It is in this context and against this background that St. Paul exhorts us to **present your bodies as a living and holy sacrifice.** Unlike the dead sacrifices of slaughtered animals, it must be a **living** sacrifice, as we live out our consecration day after day. As sacrifices were required to be unblemished, it must be **holy**, as we too strive to live unblemished and unstained by the world. Only thus can our self-oblation be **well-pleasing to God**, meet with His acceptance, and result in His blessing. Formerly, our bodies were used in the service of the devil, but now they are to be used in the service of God. This self-offering is our **rational worship**.

The words translated as *rational worship* are the Greek *logiken latreian. Latreia* is of course the usual word used to describe the cultic worship of God (see Heb. 9:1), and St. Paul uses it to describe the worship of the Temple (Rom. 9:4). Our self-oblation in the Eucharist is our *latreia* in that it is the sacrifice we offer as Christians. The sacrifices of pagans (and Jews) are carnal, consisting of the offering of dead animals. But our sacrifice is not carnal, but *logike* or **rational**—the sacrifice of our living selves. The word *logike* is cognate with the word *logos*, meaning (among other things) "word, reason, rationality." It was through His Logos (that is, His Son) that God made the world (John 1:1–3)—the Logos is the principle and Wisdom according to which all was made (see Prov. 8:22f; 1 Cor. 1:24). Our liturgical self-offering is *logike* in that it consists of immaterial and spiritual things—the sacrifice of our praise and love, our minds and hearts.

In our eucharistic worship, therefore, St. Paul exhorts us to dedicate ourselves afresh to God, uniting ourselves to Christ in His Sacrifice, walking as living members of His Body.

If we do that, we will not be **conformed to this age**. This age is ever calling on us to adapt ourselves to its *schema,* or form and outward appearance. It pressures us to look and act like everyone else in this age, to become worldly, to drop our faith and different ways of behaving. St. Paul encourages us to resist this pressure and instead be **transfigured** (Gr. *metamorphoo*, the same word used in Matt. 17:2 for the Transfiguration of Christ) by the **renewing of your mind**. We must not let our minds and mental habits become corrupt, growing old and degenerate like the world. Instead, we must let our minds be **renewed** (Gr. *anakaino*), growing fresh and brand-new (Gr. *kainos*), by dwelling on what God wills (see Eph. 4:22, 23).

Then we will **prove what is the will of God**, discerning it and doing it. The world around us, growing old and callous in sin, cannot discern such things. But we can. If we will allow our minds to be renewed by God, then we can know and recognize what is truly **good** and **well-pleasing** to Him and **perfect** (Gr. *teleios*), reaching the goal (Gr. *telos*) of pleasing the Lord.

§IV.2 Living as one member among many

3 For I say, through the grace given to me, to everyone among you, not to be high-minded beyond what you ought to mind, but to mind so as to be of sound-mind, as God divided-up to each a measure of faith.

4 For just as we have many members in one body and all members do not have the same practice,

5 thus we, who are many, are one Body in Christ and each one members of another.

6 And having *spiritual*-gifts differing according to the grace given to us, *let us use them*: if prophecy, according to the proportion of the faith;

7 **if service, in the service; or the one teaching, in the teaching;**
8 **or the one exhorting, in the exhortation; the one imparting, in simplicity; the one presiding, in eagerness; the one showing mercy, in cheerfulness.**

The apostle continues to exhort his readers. He is emphatic in his exhortation, beginning with **For I say** and drawing upon his apostolic authority, **the grace given** to him, and addressing **everyone among you**. Obviously, St. Paul feels strongly about this!—for he knows the danger of keeping aloof from one's brothers and sisters and of living independently of them. He therefore orders us **not to be high-minded beyond what you ought to mind, but to mind so as to be of sound-mind**. The sentence is difficult to translate into English, with the word *phroneo* and its cognates being used repeatedly. The word *phroneo* means "to mind, to think, to have a certain attitude or focus." We are not to **be high-minded** (Gr. *uperphroneo*) or conceited, thinking ourselves better than our neighbors. We should not think (Gr. *phroneo*) more highly of ourselves than we ought, but think and **mind** (Gr. *phroneo*) **so as to be of sound-mind**, moderate and reasonable (Gr. *sophroneo*). That is, any sense of superiority is unreasonable. God **divided-up to each a measure of faith**; each must therefore recognize in all humility that he is set in the Body as but one member, and must strive to perform his given task for the common good. God has not given all His gifts to any single person. Each one has his own allotted gift and task.

It is the same with the human body. There are **many members** in a single human body, and all those different members **do not have the same practice**, task or function (Gr. *praxis*). So also it is with the Church, the Body of Christ. We **who are many** and various, with different tasks, gifts, and functions, are still nonetheless **one Body in Christ**, so that **each one** is a **member** of the others. None can consider himself independent of the others, nor legitimately stand aloof. As members of the human body are inseparably joined together, so we too are inseparably joined to our brothers and sisters in Christ. And as members of the human body share the same biological life and care for one another, so we too must care for one another and use our gifts for mutual service and common upbuilding.

God has **divided-up** and distributed to each of us **a measure of faith**. By *faith*, the apostle does not here mean the saving faith that all Christians possess, nor the special gift of miracle-working faith given only to some (1 Cor. 12:9; 13:2). Rather, he means the individual capacity to receive spiritual gifts, which capacity God gives to different Christians in differing measures. Some Christians have the faith to receive the grace and gift of prophecy; some have enough faith to receive the gift of being a teacher; others have faith to receive the gift of exhortation. The Church has a wide variety of people in it, with a wide spectrum of **spiritual gifts** (Gr. *charismata*). Some have greater gifts (such as **prophecy** and **teaching**), and some lesser gifts (see 1 Cor. 12:28, 31, which speaks of prophecy and teaching as in the second and third place and as the greater gifts).

It may be added that there is no arbitrariness nor injustice in God's distribution of these measures of faith. There is no predestinarian fatalism in these gifts, as if some were given less faith than others apart from consideration of their responses to God. God doubtless gives more faith to those who are more fervent, and if one increases in fervency, God can add to one's measure of faith. St. Paul elsewhere exhorts Christians to "be zealous for the greater *charismata*" (1 Cor. 12:31), especially for the spiritual gift of prophecy (1 Cor. 14:2), so obviously it must be possible to receive a gift not originally given. Apparently God gives the **measure of faith** and the capacity to receive the *charismata* on the basis of the individual's desire to be used by God and his fervent prayer (see 1 Cor. 14:13).

Why, however, does St. Paul speak of God distributing to each **a measure of faith**—and not, as in Eph. 4:7, of God distributing "grace"? Because here the apostle wants to stress primarily not the variety of *the gifts themselves*, but *the capacity to receive those gifts*. Each one, he says, has received a different capacity to receive

spiritual gifts. Having received that capacity and faith, each must use it to the fullest, making the most of every opportunity to serve. One must not simply sit back and not use one's spiritual gift or **the grace given**. One must take care to utilize one's capacity and faith, receiving spiritual gifts according to one's faith.

Each person has received a different measure of faith. Some have received faith to prophesy. Let them prophesy **according to the proportion of the faith** they first received. (The Greek has the definite article—**the faith**—referring back to the "faith" previously mentioned in v. 3.) That is, let those who have received enough faith to prophesy use all that faith and prophesy at every opportunity, using that gift to the fullest.

Indeed, let everyone use his spiritual gifts according to the proportion of the measure of faith he has received. If one has received the gift of **service** or the diaconate (Gr. *diakonia*), let him use that gift in that **service**, and exercise his diaconal ministries. Let him not lose this opportunity to serve, but do the work of deacons (see 1 Tim. 3:8f).

If one has received the gift of **teaching**, let him serve in that **teaching**, missing no chance to catechize his fellows and teach the Scriptures (see Acts 13:1; Eph. 4:11).

Some may have the charisma of **exhorting**. Let this one serve in that ministry of **exhortation** (Gr. *paraklesei*). The Greek word here means not only "exhortation," but also "encouragement, urging, consolation." It refers to a ministry of counseling, strengthening the weak and the distressed.

Some have a gift of **imparting** or giving alms (Gr. *metadidomi*). These are to fulfill their tasks **in simplicity**. That is, they are not to make a big show of their alms, but to give their aid and contribution quietly, preserving the dignity of those whom they help.

Others have the gift and task of **presiding** (Gr. *proistamenos*). This indicates the work of a presbyter or elder, one of the local clergy. (The verb is used of presbyters in 1 Tim. 5:17 and of those who admonish the faithful in 1 Thess. 5:12.) They are to rule **in eagerness**, diligence and zeal (Gr. *spoude*; see its cognate verb in Titus 3:12, which translates as "to make every effort"). That is, they are not to be slack in their pastoral role, but to exert every effort, being eager to serve.

Finally, one may have the gift of **showing mercy** (Gr. *eleos*) or doing charitable works. This refers to visiting and caring for the sick, the infirm, and the imprisoned, and of burying the dead. One should do this **cheerfully** (Gr. *ilaroteti*; see its use in 2 Cor. 9:7 to describe the willing giver). Sometimes, one's charitable work for the unfortunate seems to go unappreciated by them. That should not discourage one from persevering in that holy work, nor make one grumpy or cynical in its performance. The one showing mercy must still manifest a cheerful smile, discerning the presence of the Lord in the poor and looking to His reward (Matt. 25:40).

A few things may be noted in conclusion. First of all, there is no suggestion that this list of *charismata* is meant to be exhaustive or complete, for other gifts are mentioned in 1 Cor. 12. St. Paul simply chooses seven gifts that he expects to be found in Rome for the sake of illustrating his main point, which is that one must use what one is given.

Also, we note that the *charismata* include both supernatural gifts (such as prophecy) and natural gifts (such as **imparting** or giving money). Therefore, charismatic gifts are not by definition supernatural, and the charismatic designation should not be confined to the more sensational gifts, such as prophecy and tongues.

Lastly, we note too that St. Paul includes in his list gifts that traditionally require ordination (such as the gift of **ruling**, exercised by presbyters), as well as gifts that do not require ordination (such as the gift of **showing mercy**). It is illegitimate therefore to oppose the charismatic to the institutional. In the "institution" of the Church, all gifts are "charismatic," and there is no dichotomy between them. For "all good giving and every perfect gift is from above, coming down from You, the Father of lights" (from the Prayer before the Ambo). All that we have comes from Him.

§IV.3 Living in love

> ॐ ॐ ॐ ॐ ॐ
>
> 9 ***Let*** **love** ***be*** **unhypocritical; abhor the evil; cling to the good.**

St. Paul continues to exhort us to live the transfigured life. He has called us to an attitude of sober humility, using our gifts to serve one another as fellow-members of the same Body. He now calls us to let love characterize all that service.

Sounding the keynote, he urges us to let our Christian **love** (Gr. *agape*) be **unhypocritical** and genuine. Certainly as disciples of the Lord of love, we strive to walk in love toward all men. The challenge is to let this love be **unhypocritical** (Gr. *anupokritos*; see the "hypocrites" of Matt. 23:13f). The word *hypocrite* comes originally from the Greek, meaning literally "to answer"; it eventually came to connote the dialogue of the stage, and finally, acting in the worst sense. The *upokritos* is one who simply plays a part, pretending to devotion he does not have. St. Paul says that our love must not be feigned, but must come from the heart and the will. We must not say sweet words to our neighbor's face and then curse and deride him after he turns away.

Such genuineness is possible only as we maintain our integrity and love the truth. We must **abhor the evil**, utterly rejecting such double-dealing as disgusting behavior, unworthy of our high calling; and we must **cling to the good**. It is as the Lord said: such prevarication and two-facedness come from the evil one (Matt. 5:37). Uprightness and love of the light are to be the root and source of our mutual love.

> ॐ ॐ ॐ ॐ ॐ
>
> 10 **With brotherly-love, warmly-love one another; go before one another in** ***showing*** **honor;**

Having spoken of the *agape* which should characterize our dealings with all men, St. Paul exhorts us to special warmth of affection in our dealings with our Christian brothers and fellow-members with whom we share the eucharistic chalice. We should deal with them as true comrades and friends, having **brotherly-love** (Gr. *philadelphia*) in our hearts. Fulfilling the word of the Psalmist, we must be true brothers (Gr. *adelphoi*) dwelling together (Ps. 133:1 LXX), letting no quarrel come between us. We should **warmly-love one another**, and strive to **go before** our neighbors, to take the lead **in showing honor** to them. Far from picking out the best seats for ourselves at feasts (see Luke 14:7), we will give place to our neighbor and delight to heap honor upon him.

The word translated here *warmly-love* is the Greek *philostorgeo*. It is cognate with the word used in 4 Maccabees 15:9 to describe the strong feelings of tenderness that the Maccabean mother had for her seven sons as they were being cruelly martyred for their faith. It is also connected with the word *storge*, which denotes the warmth of family feeling. The apostle therefore exhorts his hearers to warmly embrace one another as they would their closest kin.

11 do not be lazy in eagerness; be boiling in the Spirit, serving *as slaves to* the Lord;

This love is to be manifested in concrete deeds. We are not to be **lazy** or let our **eagerness** flag or fall behind. The word translated *eagerness* is the same word used in 12:8 and in Titus 3:12, where it denotes determined diligence. We are not to let this eager zeal tire out, but are to expend every effort in serving one another. We are, in fact, to **be boiling in the Spirit**. The word translated *boil* is the Greek *zeo*, meaning "to seethe." It is the word used in Job 32:19 LXX to describe wine boiling—and in 4 Maccabees 18:20, to describe the seething rage of Antiochus against the Maccabees. Christians are also to seethe and burn—not with rage, but with the fire of the Spirit. We are to let the fire of the Spirit of God burn brightly within us, empowering us in our mutual service. This we can easily do, for we are not **serving** ***as slaves*** to mere men, but to **the Lord**. He it is who receives our deeds of service to our neighbors, and He it is who will reward us (see Col. 3:23, 24). (The term *Spirit* used here refers most likely to the Holy Spirit and not to the human spirit, since it is paired with *the Lord*.)

12 rejoicing in hope; persevering in tribulation; attached to prayer;

The Lord will indeed reward us on the Last Day. Therefore we can **rejoice in hope**. We are not to allow our present sufferings to weigh us down, but are to **rejoice** and exult in our worship, certain of our final victory. We are to **persevere** in the **tribulation** that will come and not be discouraged or give up on God. On the contrary, we are to be **attached to prayer** (see Rom. 8:26).

The word translated *attached to* is the Greek *proskartereo*. It is the word used in Acts 8:13 for Simon the sorcerer, when he attached himself (almost bodily!) to St. Philip; and in Acts 10:7 for the servants who were in constant attendance upon Cornelius the centurion. In the same way, St. Paul tells us, we should make prayer our constant occupation. We should look for every spare moment to pray, taking every available opportunity to turn to God. Then we will truly "pray without ceasing" (1 Thess. 5:17).

13 contributing to the needs of the saints; seeking ***opportunities to practice*** **hospitality.**

As well, we are not to let suffering make us withdraw into our own little ghetto of safety. We are to **contribute to the needs of the saints**, the fellow believers. Especially in times of persecution, believers can fall into great want. The apostle exhorts us to be zealous in relieving those needs whenever we can. Should any believers come our way, for example, driven as they might be by their distress, we should open our homes to them, practicing **hospitality** and the love of strangers (Gr. *philoxenia*). As the proverb says, "All roads lead to Rome," and should any weary traveler walk that road to the Roman Christians' homes, they should find a warm Christian welcome.

14 Bless the ones persecuting you—bless and do not curse!

For persecution will inevitably come to all who love the Lord (see John 15:20). St. Paul is emphatic that we must **bless the ones persecuting** us. Indeed, he repeats his order twice, and again in negative form: **bless and do not curse**! This is what the Lord commanded too (Matt. 5:44). In the proud and cold world around us, hostility is met with counter-hostility and retaliation is the inevitable order of the day. In blessing our enemies and meeting hostility with love, we will show ourselves to be truly not of this world. Like our Lord's, our manifestation of a supernatural humility shows all that our true citizenship is in heaven.

15 Rejoice with the ones who rejoice, weep with the ones who weep.
16 Mind the same thing toward one another; do not mind high *things*, but be carried-off to lowly *things*. Do not be prudent in your own *eyes*.

And this response of humility must be carried over into all our life. Our call is to **rejoice with the ones who rejoice** and to **weep with the ones who weep**.

It is easy to be haughty, like the world. The world's "macho" attitude is rooted in pride, and this is to be far from those who follow Him who humbled Himself even to the death of the Cross. Instead, we should **mind the same thing toward one another** and have the same attitude as our neighbor. That is, we should live in harmony, all of us together striving to preserve our unity of heart. We should not **mind high *things***, being **prudent** and wise in our **own eyes**. We should not disdain our more humble brothers, regarding them as stupid and inferior. Rather, we should **be carried-off to lowly *things***.

The verb translated *carried-off* is the Greek *sunapago*. It is the verb used by Paul in Galatians 2:13, when he says that even Barnabas was "carried-off" by the Judaizers' hypocrisy; and by Peter in 2 Peter 3:17, when he warns against being "carried-off" by the error of unprincipled men. The thought here is of not resisting when circumstances lead one to lowly places, to work with the lowly as one of them. One should not think of oneself as too good for such poor people, fearing to dirty one's hands by being among them and sharing their lot. On the contrary, one should willingly and enthusiastically join in with them.

17 Render no one wickedness for wickedness. Take forethought for what is right before all men.

18 If able, as it is from you *yourselves*, be at peace with all men.

19 Do not avenge yourselves, beloved, but give place to the wrath, for it is written, "Mine is *the* avenging, I *Myself* will render!" says *the* Lord.

20 "But if your enemy hungers, feed him; if he thirsts, *give* him drink, for doing this, charcoals of fire you will heap-up upon his head!"

21 Do not be conquered by the wicked, but conquer the wicked by the good.

If we have this otherworldly humility and supernatural love, one that will return blessings for curses, then we will also **render no one wickedness for wickedness**. The world, St. Paul says, may treat us shabbily, but we must return kindness. Instead of quickly lashing back when insulted, we should **take forethought for what is right before all men**. Rather than instantly responding, we must first think, "How will this response commend the Gospel to the world?" If it will cause the world to further revile the Christians, we should simply absorb the insult meekly and be quiet. Thus, we will **be at peace with all men**. (St. Paul is, of course, a realist, and realizes that sometimes it is simply not possible to maintain harmony with all. Some people will insist on a fight, and there is nothing anyone can do about it! That is why he prefaces his exhortation by saying **if able, as it is from you**—insofar as it depends on us, we should live in peace. For sometimes it does *not* depend upon us, but the quarrelsome man will have his quarrel.)

But either way, we must **not avenge ourselves** when we are insulted, hurt, or persecuted. Knowing how difficult a thing this is, he addresses us tenderly as **beloved**. But we must still resist the temptation to lash out in return. Rather, we may **give place to the wrath** of God. The desire to avenge oneself is motivated by fear—fear that perhaps the injustice will go unavenged, that the evil man will get away with his wickedness. We need not fear. We must trust God's justice, for no one ultimately gets away with anything. "God is not mocked" (Gal. 6:7), but will give to all as they deserve.

We may be sure of this, for **it is written** in the Scriptures (Deut. 32:35). **"Mine is *the* avenging, I *Myself* will render!" says *the* Lord.** The *Mine* is emphatic in the Greek, standing at the head of the sentence, and the *I* is emphatic also (Gr. *ego*). Thus, we are not to avenge ourselves, for that would be to usurp the place of God! It is *His* task to mete out final vengeance and render eternal justice.

What then is *our* task? **"If your enemy hungers, feed him; if he thirsts, give him drink, for doing this, charcoals of fire you will heap-up upon his head!"** (a paraphrase of Prov. 25:21, 22). That is, returning kindness for hostility is the perfect revenge and the most appropriate response. Just as one would conquer and defeat one's foe if one heaped fiery coals on his head, so our wicked enemy will be effectively **conquered** by doing him **good**. For through the goodness done in return, he may repent and cease to be an enemy. In the world, the invariable response is to take one's own revenge and to strike down one's enemy if one comes upon him when he is vulnerable. That is the way to conquer and deal with one's foes! But that is not Christ's way. For the Christian, the way not to **be conquered by the wicked** is not to hurt him in return, but rather to **conquer** him **by the good.**

This may seem unrealistic to the world, as if the Church lived in a kind of Pollyanna fantasy land. But it has proven to be sober and practical truth. Human history and experience teach that when men give in to hatred and the urge to strike back in retaliation, the evil within them does more harm to them than it does to their victims. Anger and the lust for vengeance eat a man up inside, leaving him nothing but a hollow, raging shell. It may seem initially as if these words of nonretaliation to hurt and insult come from one intent on not facing reality. But the opposite is the case. St. Paul knows what anger can do and how it works like a cancer on the human heart (see Acts 9:1, 2). And, taught by the Lord, he knows too that a man's only hope for emerging unscathed from the battle lies in not letting that hatred lodge within.

§IV.4 Living in submission to the state

13 1 **Let every soul be in submission to surpassing authorities, for there is no authority except by God, and the ones that are have been appointed by God.**

2 **Therefore the one who opposes the authority has withstood the ordinance of God, and they who have withstood will receive judgment upon themselves.**

In his previous exhortations about never avenging oneself, St. Paul is speaking of responding to private insults and abuse, not to criminal acts. His basic directive is that the Christians should live in peace (see 12:18). This is especially so in their relationship with the secular state. If the believers are truly to "take forethought for what is right" in the sight of all men (12:17), they must also be seen by all not to be unruly or rebellious.

So it is that St. Paul exhorts **every soul** to **be in submission** to the **surpassing** and highly placed civil **authorities**. The apostle's emphasis can be seen in his exhorting **every soul** (Gr. *psuche*)—that is, every single one having life. If one is alive, he is included in this apostolic directive and should listen!

For the temptation is for the Christian to think that, because through his faith he transcends this pagan world, he possesses some heavenly diplomatic immunity from civil law. But the believer must not think of himself as *above* the civil law. Actually, he must know himself as *in submission* to it, living *below* it and under its jurisdiction.

For even though civil rulers were, in St. Paul's time, all pagan, they were (and are) nonetheless part of God's providential plan for ordering and blessing the world. **No authority** of government exists **except by God** and His will, and all **the ones that are have been appointed by God**. What God has **appointed** and put up (Gr. *tasso*), men should not **oppose** and put down (Gr. *antitasso*). Given the bribery, violence, scheming, and sometimes murder with which men sometimes come to power, this truth is not immediately apparent. But it is true nonetheless. God has permitted in His Providence all that is, and has ordered it as He wills. The civil authorities—even the bad ones—are His doing, so that if one rebelliously reviles and seeks to overthrow social order, one has actually **withstood the ordinance of God**. The anarchist will there **receive judgment** and punishment from God, for he has actually opposed not just men, but also God Himself.

3 For rulers are not a *cause of* fear to the good

work, but to the wicked. Do you will to have no fear of authority? Do the good, and you will have praise from it,
4 **for it is a servant of God to you for the good. But if you do the wickedness, fear, for it does not bear the sword in vain, for it is a servant of God, an avenger for wrath upon the one who practices wickedness.**

The anarchist will receive judgment from God, for government and civil order are good. The Christians should not fear their **rulers** even if they are pagan, for the rulers are **not a *cause of* fear** for those practicing **the good work** and law-abiding behavior, but only for **the wicked** and criminal. If the Christians **do the good** and show proper respect for the law, they will **have praise** and approval from their rulers, for the ruler is **a servant of God** to them for their **good** and benefit. The rulers want what is best for the common good and the peace. If one disturbs that peace, however, by criminal and **wicked** acts, then one should **fear** the authorities, for the ruler **does not bear the sword in vain**. Crimes will receive their proper and just punishment.

For the ruler is in this instance the true **servant of God** (Gr. *diakonos*), carrying out His righteous will **for wrath** as **an avenger** of the **one who practices wickedness**. The civil retribution exacted from the criminal is not state tyranny—it is the work and sentence of God upon the evildoer, and His provision for restraining evil in the world. For it is in part through His servants, the secular rulers, that God's authority is manifested in the earth.

5 **Therefore it is necessary to be in submission, not only because of the wrath, but also because of the conscience.**

Because of this, it is **necessary** for the Christian **to be in**

submission to these rulers—**not only because of the wrath** of the state, when it punishes crime, **but also because of the conscience.** That is, the believer must be law-abiding, not simply to avoid prosecution and the suffering inflicted by the state, but also because God commands it. By his law-abiding behavior, the Christian not only obeys the state and wins its approval, but he also obeys God, and wins His.

6 **For because of this you also pay taxes, for they**
are God's offerers, devoting themselves to this
very thing.
7 **Render to all their due: tax to whom tax, cus-**
tom to whom custom, fear to whom fear, honor
to whom honor.

It is exactly **because of this**—that the ruler does the will of God as His servant—that we also **pay taxes**. That is, the state's collection of money is not simply a form of legalized robbery, whereby the strong take from the weak. Rather, it is the state's lawful and just reward, as those who serve God and carry out His will. They are **God's offerers**. The word translated here *offerer* is the Greek *leitourgos*, the same word used in the Greek Old Testament to describe the priests who attend to the sacrificial service of God. By using the term here, St. Paul means to show that the civil rulers serve God as truly as do His religious priests, each in their separate spheres. As the priests do their sacrificial and cultic work and receive certain parts of the sacrifices as their due reward (see 1 Cor. 9:13), so too the rulers receive taxes as their own due. The priests diligently perform their task, and the rulers too **devote themselves** (Gr. *proskartereo*; see its use in 12:12) **to this very thing**.

The Christians then must **render** and pay back to all **their due**, giving them what is justly owed, both from the pocket and from the heart. One should pay whatever **tax** is levied on persons or lands, and whatever **custom** or toll might be exacted from the traveler.

One should render the proper **fear** and respect to those members of high and noble rank (who could exact punishment if disrespect were showed) and also the proportionate **honor** to those of lesser rank (who lacked the means of punishing disrespectful behavior). That is, one should pay all one's social debts, giving to each one exactly as he is entitled. Whether taxes when at home or tolls when traveling, whether the required prostration to the great or a mere bow to those of lesser station, the believer should submissively give to all the secular servants of God their due—because they are the servants of God.

(One final note: All the above deals only with the basic Christian commitment to be good and law-abiding citizens and to avoid anarchic treason. The vexed question of what to do under an evil regime with its evil laws is not in view here. It is a misapplication of St. Paul's thought to read this as if it dealt with the question of whether civil disobedience or a *coup d'etat* is ever allowed.)

§IV.5 Summary: Love as the fulfillment of the Law at the end of the age

8 Be a debtor to no one, except to love one another, for he who loves the other has fulfilled *the* Law.

9 For this, "You shall not commit adultery, You shall not murder, You shall not steal, You shall not desire," and if *there is any* other commandment, it is headed-up in this word, "You shall love your neighbor as yourself."

10 The love works no wickedness to the neighbor; therefore the love is *the* fullness of *the* Law.

Having spoken of the necessity of paying taxes owing, St. Paul takes a wider view, telling us that we should not only not be a debtor to the tax-collector, but should **be a debtor to no one**. The thought here is not that we should never incur debt, but rather that we must not refuse to pay back our debts once we have incurred them. "The wicked man borrows and does not repay" (Ps. 37:21), but we must repay as we can.

There is one debt, however, which we can never fully discharge: the debt to **love one another**.

In paying off debts, there is always relief when the debt is discharged, that we need have nothing to do with our debtor again. We now owe him nothing, and we can sweep him from our life! Then, if we wish, we may with impunity pretend that we do not know him when we see him in the street. The discharging of debts can sometimes lead to a certain self-isolation on our parts.

It is this self-isolation that St. Paul warns against as something disastrous for the soul. We must indeed repay our debts—but not because we wish to sever our connections with our neighbor, or aspire to self-sufficient independence. On the contrary, this life-giving connection must remain forever, binding our hearts in love to our neighbor. Unlike other debts, this debt we may pay time and again without diminishing the need to repay. With other debts, each time for repayment brings closer the time when we will owe nothing. But not the debt of love: this we will owe forever. For, as St. Anthony the Great said, "Our life and death is with our neighbor."

Once again, St. Paul casts a quick look over his shoulder at his Judaizing opponent, and says that **he who loves has fulfilled *the* Law**. His Jewish opponent insisted that the Law must be fulfilled and that it is fulfilled through keeping its rules about circumcision, Sabbaths, and food laws. For St. Paul, the one who loves has completely fulfilled the intent of the Law, apart from such rules. That is because such precepts as "**You shall not commit adultery, You shall not murder, You shall not steal, You shall not desire**" or covet—or, indeed, ***any* other commandment** they could mention—are all **headed-up** and embodied in the single commandment, "**You shall love your neighbor as yourself.**"

This **word** or directive from Lev. 19:18 thus could function as a condensation of the entire Law. It is as Rabbi Hillel said, when challenged to teach the entire Law while standing on one foot: "'What is hurtful to you, do not do to others.' That is the whole

Law—all else is commentary." Similarly, St. Paul here boils all the Law down to one precept—the positive commandment to love one's neighbor. If one walks by this love, one will **work no wickedness** to the **neighbor** spoken of in that precept. And how can one be blamed if one does no harm to those around? Therefore that **love** is truly ***the* fullness of *the* Law.**

Note, the apostle does *not* say that love is "the *fulfillment* of the Law." He says something stronger: that it is the *fullness* of the Law (Gr. *pleroma*; see its use in Gal. 4:4; Eph. 3:19; Col. 1:19). In other words, all that the Law contains, all its life-giving teaching and power, is in love. If one has love, one has all the reality contained in the Law. That is why the one who loves has already fulfilled the Law's inner demands—and why love remains the eternal debt which we will ever delight to pay to our neighbor.

11 And *do* this, knowing the *appointed* time, that it is already *the* hour for you to awaken out of sleep, for now our salvation *is* nearer than when we *first* had faith.
12 The night is advanced and the day has drawn near. Let us therefore put off the works of darkness and put on the weapons of light.
13 Let us walk properly as in *the* day, not in revels and *bouts of* drunkenness, not in beds and sensuality, not in strife and jealousy,
14 but put on the Lord Jesus Christ and do not take forethought for the flesh, for *its* desires.

We should **do this**—living in love—**knowing the *appointed* time** (Gr. *kairos*) and appreciating the eschatological season in which we dwell. Every new day brings our **salvation** even **nearer**, as the Lord's Second Coming relentlessly draws near, and from the time when we first put our **faith** in Christ until now, the eschatological clock has continued to tick. This relentless approach of Christ means that every day brings with it a sense of moral urgency. The days are evil, and we must buy up every opportunity to do good (see Eph. 5:16). It is **already *the* hour** to **awaken out of sleep** and out of the slothful slumber of sin. Every day that we continue in moral lethargy brings us another day closer to eternal disaster.

That is because the long dark **night** of this age is well **advanced**; the new **day** of the age to come has **drawn near** and is even now at hand (see Phil. 4:5). The imminence of the Second Coming colors all the remaining days of this dying and closing age.

In those days, labor began at dawn, and few workers would remain in bed after the sun's rays lightened the sky. Just before the dawn, the worker would rise up, put off his coverlet and begin his labors. In the same way, now that the **night** of this present age is **advanced** and almost over, and the new **day** of the age to come has **drawn near**, we too must **awaken out of sleep** and rise up. Like soldiers on duty, we must **put off** the coverlet under which we lay throughout the night and **put on** our **weapons**—not the worldly weapons of breastplate, helmet, and sword for warfare against physical foes, but the **weapons of light** for warfare against a spiritual enemy.

When we lay in the dark night of this age, we lay sleeping and heedless under the coverlet of sin. Now that the day of the age to come is at hand, we must **put off** those **works of darkness**. Now that the night is all but finished, we must **walk properly** and decently, as befits those walking **in the day**. Night is the time for **revels** and rowdy parties, for ***bouts of*** **drunkenness**, with **strife and jealousy**, for **beds** of fornication and for shameless **sensuality**. Such enormities are done under cover of darkness—not in the broad light of day! (See 1 Thess. 5:7.) Now that the day is arriving, we must throw off such **works of darkness** and have done with them once and for all. Like children of the light, we must **put on weapons of light** and reject such behavior, making war against it as we would against an enemy.

More than that, we must **put on the Lord Jesus Christ**—He who is Himself the eternal Light and splendor of our souls. Before, when we were pagans, we took pleasure in such things. Now our pleasure is in the Lord. *He* is our armor and victory over our old way, and having clothed ourselves with Him at our baptism

(Gal. 3:27), we can triumph over the ways of the flesh. Thus we must not **take forethought for the flesh** or arrange how we might fulfill its unbridled and unlawful **desires**. The time for our concern for finding the next rowdy debauch is over. Now our concern is for the Lordship of Jesus Christ in our lives and for fulfilling *His* will. As children of the day, we are consecrated to Him.

EXCURSUS:

ON THE IMMINENCE OF THE SECOND COMING

Throughout the New Testament, there breathes the constant expectation of the Lord's return. The day of that Coming has "drawn near" (Rom. 13:12), the Lord is "near" (Phil. 4:5), the Coming of the Lord has "drawn near" (James 5:8), as has "the end of all things" (1 Pet. 4:7). Thus, it is "the last hour" (1 John 3:18). The question may be asked, therefore: Did the apostles believe that the Lord would return in their lifetime?

Though it is often stated that the apostles did believe this (and certainly some in the first generation did believe it, see 2 Thess. 2:2), there are other apostolic texts to be weighed as well. Side by side with these assertions that the Second Coming is imminent are other assertions that it is not to be expected soon. In 2 Thessalonians (one of his earliest letters), St. Paul specifically cautions his readers *not* to expect the Lord's return until after certain events have occurred, such as the collapse of the social order and the rise of the Antichrist—none of which events was remotely on the horizon. Also, in his Epistle to the Romans, the apostle cites the conversion of Israel as one of the signs that will precede the Lord's Coming (Rom. 11:25, 26)—and this too showed no sign of beginning to occur.

In dealing with the delay of the Second Coming, St. Peter cites the principle that "with the Lord, one day is as a thousand years and a thousand years as one day"

(2 Pet. 3:8) to show that God does not measure time as men do. In the Gospels themselves (committed to writing later than the Epistles), St. Luke records one of the Lord's parables which He told because some "supposed that the Kingdom of God was going to appear immediately" (Luke 19:11). In this parable, the Lord speaks of a certain nobleman who "went to a distant country to receive a kingdom for himself" and who told his servants to "do business until he returned" (vv. 12, 13). The great distance traveled and the necessity of his servants conducting business until his return speak of a long absence. This in itself militates against the notion that the Lord would return immediately.

What then are we to make of these varied voices? It would seem that, in apostolic times, the Lord's return was imminent not in the chronological sense of calendar years, but from the eschatological perspective of the ages. All of history had been preparing for Christ and His Kingdom, and now at last "the ends of the ages have come" (1 Cor. 10:11). The Lord had been crucified, buried, risen and ascended—and now was ready to return. His Second Coming was "near" in the sense that no great and long unfolding of civilization need occur before it should happen. The "last hour" had come, the last item on the divine and eternal agenda of the ages had been reached. Israel had been regathered from the Exile and placed in the land; Messiah had come and accomplished His work, taking away the sins of the world. He had ascended on high and was reigning over the world. All that was left was His final return and triumph. The signs preceding that return (see Luke 21:25, 26; 2 Thess. 2:3) could occur without any warning, in any generation.

It was in this sense that His Coming was near and ever at hand. The urgency accompanying that Coming was not the urgency of the almanac or the calendar, but of the human heart awaiting the return of the Beloved (Song 8:14; Rev. 22:17, 20).

V

LIVING TOGETHER IN A MIXED JEWISH–GENTILE COMMUNITY (14:1—15:13)

The apostle now deals with another aspect of the Romans' life of love together as a Christian community—the tensions of living as a mixed group of Jews and Gentiles.

It is apparent that St. Paul is not dealing with any theological concerns or heresies, such as vexed the Galatian churches. In Galatia, a Judaizing heresy had begun to take root, which said that a Christian must keep the Jewish Law to be saved. Such was not the case in Rome. Some in Rome felt that they should keep certain holy days, but they did not do so as a matter of necessity, nor did they suggest that everyone must keep those days in order to be saved. They kept certain food laws as a matter of scrupulosity and conscience, but they did not say that all must do so. The situation in Rome was therefore quite different from that in Galatia, and St. Paul accordingly takes a more flexible stance. Since these practices were observed as matters of individual preference, they might be allowed to stand. The issue was how people who observed different individual practices could still live together in harmony. All concerned admitted that these things were matters of indifference as regards salvation. But how to combine them in one community? In particular, how could they preserve table fellowship together? That was the issue before the apostle as he gave thought to their life together.

14 1 **Now the one who is weak in faith take in, but not for discernment of questionings.**

2 One indeed has faith that he may eat all things,
but he who is weak eats vegetables.
3 Let not him who eats disdain the one who does
not eat, and let not him who does not eat judge
him who eats, for God has taken him in.
4 Who are you to judge the house-*slave* of another? To his lord he stands *firm* or falls; and
he will be made to stand, for the Lord is able
to make him stand.
5 One judges a day above *another* day; one judges
every day *alike*. Let each be fully-assured in his
own mind.
6 He who minds the day, minds *it* to *the* Lord,
and he who eats, eats to *the* Lord, for he *gives*
thanksgiving to God; and he who does not eat,
does not eat to *the* Lord, and *gives* thanksgiving to God.
7 For no one of us lives to himself and no one
dies to himself,
8 for if we live, to the Lord we live, or if we die,
to the Lord we die. Therefore whether we live
or die, we are the Lord's.
9 For to this *end* Christ died and lived, that He
might be lord both of the dead and the living.

St. Paul distinguishes between two types of people—the one who is **weak in faith** and the one who is strong. The weaker one is characterized by what would later be called "scruples," or an overly sensitive conscience. This one feels uneasy and guilty if certain rules are not followed. He perhaps has a more tentative grasp on the truth that God loves him just as he is, and feels obliged to observe certain practices. As said above, this is not a matter of having to observe these practices in order to be saved (as was the contention in the Galatian churches). It is more that he feels uneasy and haunted by a guilty conscience.

What are some of these practices? St. Paul singles out two of them as examples. First of all, though the stronger brother **has faith that he may eat all things**, including meat, **he who is weak eats vegetables** only. It is unlikely that the issue is about meat offered to idols, for the apostle's position here is that *no one* is allowed to eat what he knows has been offered to idols (see 1 Cor. 8—10). And vegetarianism is not characteristic of Judaism in itself. Perhaps, however, some in Rome were so afraid of inadvertently eating meat that had been offered to idols that in order to avoid all possibility of mistake, they avoided *all* meat. The Jewish community of the Essenes had adopted a vegetarian diet, and perhaps some felt that this was the safer route in order to avoid the very possibility of contamination.

Secondly, St. Paul mentions that though the stronger brother **judges** and esteems **every day *alike***, the weaker brother **judges a day above *another*** as more important. Thus some days (perhaps Sabbaths and holy days) were esteemed by him as more propitious than others or as entailing the performance of special obligations.

Whatever the specific nature of the scruples felt by the weaker brother, St. Paul enjoins the church at large to **take** him **in** and welcome him warmly—**but not for discernment of questionings**. That is, the church must not receive the weaker brother solely in order to debate with him and pass judgment on his opinions. They must not begin to sift through his scruples or start arguments, looking down upon him and **disdaining** him. Nor, in this context of mutual analysis and debate, must the weaker brother **judge** the other, thinking him insensitive and impious. He too must **take him in**—since **God has taken him in**. If God has welcomed him, then he must do so too. Neither the weak nor the strong must judge or condemn the other.

To judge a brother over such trifles would be as ludicrous as one **judging the house-*slave*** of another. Obviously no one has the right to go into another man's home and tell his household staff how to behave! It is **to his** own **lord** and master that the house-slave **stands or falls**. His own master is the only one fit to judge his performance. And it is the same with the Church. It is up to the Lord Jesus alone to say whether a brother **stands** in His favor or **falls** into disfavor—and that brother **will be made to stand, for the Lord is able to make him stand**. That is, the Lord, risen and interceding at the right hand of God, will acknowledge him at the Last Judgment, so that he will not be condemned over such unimportant externals.

Thus, each one must be **fully-assured in his own mind**. For as long as he does what he does to please the Lord, it will meet with His divine approval. **He who minds the day** and keeps it as special does so **to *the* Lord**, in order to honor Him. And the one **who eats** all things, also does so **to *the* Lord** and for His sake. This is apparent, since he **gives thanksgiving to God**. He is not eating merely to please himself and satisfy his appetite for meat, but as a part of his dedication to the Lord, and his eating glorifies Him. It is the same with him **who does not eat**, for he also refrains as **to *the* Lord** and equally **gives thanksgiving to God** for his food. In both cases, the lives of the different brothers are dedicated to the Lord.

This is fitting, since **no one lives to himself and no one dies to himself**. We none of us belong ultimately to ourselves, but only to God. Thus all of our actions must be referred to Him—and can only be judged by Him. All of our lives—all of our choices, our deeds, even our dying—must be referred **to the Lord** and be done for His sake. The center of our existence must be Him, not our own will. We live and will die solely for His pleasure and glory. **Whether we live or die, we are the Lord's** and belong to Him.

That is, in fact, the reason **Christ died and lived**, enduring the Cross and rising again—that He **might be lord both of the dead and the living**. That is, His death and Resurrection happened that He might rule over all, extending His sovereignty even over the dead. As the Lord over all, obviously *He* must be the reference-point for all of our lives—not our own little rules and preferences. Thus, since He is Lord, if someone does something to honor Him, that act is honorable and may not be judged by us.

10 But you, why do you judge your brother? Or you also, why do you disdain your brother?

For we shall all be made to stand-before the judgment-seat of God.
11 For it is written, "*As* I Myself live, says the Lord, that to Me every knee will bend and every tongue will confess to God."
12 So then, each one of us will give a word concerning himself to God.
13 Therefore let us not judge one another any longer, but judge this rather, not to put an obstacle before the brother or a stumbling-block.

The apostle again hammers his point home, asking pointedly: **You** there—yes, you! (The word *you* leads the sentence in the Greek.) You weaker brother, judging your neighbor's liberty—**why do you judge your brother**? And **you also**! You stronger brother, looking down upon him in return, as if he were a silly fool—**why do you disdain your brother**? For **we shall all**—strong and weak alike—**be made to stand-before the judgment-seat of God**; then and only then will come the time for passing judgment—and we will not be the ones passing it!

The word translated *judgment-seat* is the Greek word *bema*, the word used for the Roman tribunal, the throne from which cases were heard and justice dispensed (see Matt. 27:19; Acts 18:12). St. Paul uses it here for the final and divine Tribunal, before which all men must one day stand and before which all must one day give account. Men trembled to stand before the Roman *bema*—how much more will they tremble to stand before the *bema* of the Most High? That judgment will come soon enough, and we may not anticipate it by condemning our brother as if *we* were the final judges.

This may be seen in the Scripture that St. Paul cites, paraphrasing Isaiah 45:23. In its original context, this was a prophecy of the day when God's sovereignty would be unchallenged in all the earth, as every tongue swore allegiance to God and all rebellion was overcome. In fact, this day will only come when Jesus returns, and so St. Paul refers this prophecy's fulfillment to the time when **every knee will bend** before His divine judgment-seat at the Second Coming and **every tongue confess to God** its hidden deeds. It is then that **each one of us** will **give a word** and account of himself **to God**. It is thus to Him and to Him alone that each one of us will give that account—not to one another.

We must therefore let God be the judge of all and not usurp His divine prerogatives by **judging one another**. If any want to "judge" and utter decisions, then let them **judge this rather** and decide this: **not to put an obstacle** before their brother. Here is a worthy decision for any who would play the judge! Since they are so discerning, let them discern this! For to judge and condemn their brother would indeed be to place a **stumbling-block** before him, to trip him up and stop him from following the Lord.

14 I know and have been persuaded in *the* Lord Jesus that nothing is common through itself, except to the one reckoning anything to be common—to that one, *it is* common.
15 For if because of food your brother is made sorrowful, you are no longer walking according to love. Do not by your food destroy that one for whom Christ died.
16 Therefore do not let your good be slandered,
17 for the Kingdom of God is not eating and drinking, but righteousness and peace and joy in *the* Holy Spirit.
18 For he who in this *way* serves the Christ *as a slave* is well-pleasing to God and approved by men.

The apostle continues to examine these issues in greater detail. With great conviction, he states that he **knows and has been persuaded in the Lord Jesus** that no food is in itself **common**, or unsanctified and unclean. **Except**, of course, to **the one reckoning** it to be so—to him indeed ***it is* common** and unclean. That is, what is decisive in these matters is the conscience of the individual. Through his union with the Lord and by observing Christ's own example (see Mark 7:1–23), St. Paul can state categorically that food is simply food and that **through** and in itself, it cannot spiritually contaminate one. But if one eats that same food with a bad conscience, so that by eating it one is inwardly forsaking his dedication to Christ, *then* it is common and unclean *to him*—not in itself, but through the work of his conscience.

The stronger brothers should therefore take care. If they debate with their weaker brother and persuade him, against his own conscience, to eat with **sorrow** what he feels is wrong, then that weaker brother will violate his conscience and his loyalty to Christ and thus be **destroyed**. This is not fulfilling their acknowledged goal of **walking according to love**! **Christ died** for that brother—how can they destroy one whom the Lord died to save from destruction, and all for mere **food**?

Their liberty to eat all things is **good**. But they should use their liberty with care, not forcing their freedom unseasonably on their weaker brothers, to their destruction. If they do that, no one will praise their liberty as good; rather, they will then **slander** it as a source of disunity and harm.

For after all, what matters, the essence of **the Kingdom of God**, is not such passing externals as **eating and drinking**. Rather, the Kingdom consists of such abiding inner realities as **righteousness and peace and joy in *the* Holy Spirit**. Therefore, let them pursue this inner transformation given by the Holy Spirit. Let them be concerned for true righteousness, shunning impurity and lawlessness (see 6:19), and not be obsessed over such trifles as what they eat at a meal. Let them pursue peace with all men, avoiding quarrels with their weaker brothers. Let them rejoice in the Lord and preserve His joy within them, and not darken their days with senseless debates. The Kingdom of God consists in these inner realities, not in such externals as they are debating. They should therefore not let these externals loom so large that they are prepared to let their **good** liberty be **slandered** because of them.

If they will **in this *way***—the way of concern for their brother—

serve the Christ ***as a slave*** (Gr. *douleuo*, cognate with *doulos*, "slave"), then their good will not be rejected as evil. On the contrary, in addition to being **well-pleasing to God**, they will be **approved by men**, and their liberty will be seen as the good thing it is.

19 So then let us pursue the things of peace and the things for building up one another.
20 Do not for the sake of food tear down the work of God. All things indeed *are* clean, but *they are* wicked for the man *who* by eating causes stumbling.
21 *It is* well not to eat meat nor to drink wine nor *do* anything in which your brother stumbles.
22 *The* faith which you have, have according to yourself before God. Blessed is the one who does not judge himself in what he approves!
23 But he who doubts has been condemned if he eats, because it is not out of faith. All that is not out of faith is sin.

The apostle begins to sum up, saying, **let us pursue the things of peace and the things for building up one another**. The Romans should simply welcome newcomers as they are and not strive to make them change their ways. If a quarrel seems to threaten, let them break it off and pursue, not victory in the debate, but rather **peace** between themselves. Let them strive to build others up spiritually, giving them what they actually need, not forcing on them their own ideas. To force the convictions of their own stronger conscience upon their weaker brothers is to **tear down** the very **work of God**—which work they should be helping to **build up**—and all for the sake of mere **food**! This invites God's retribution upon the one who sacrilegiously tears down what He has labored to build. Let the stronger brother beware!

In speaking to the stronger brother, St. Paul admits that **all things**

indeed *are* clean in themselves and that the stronger brother is free to eat and drink whatever he wants, including the **meat** which the weaker brother avoids. But these things become **wicked** for him if **by eating** them he would **cause stumbling** to his weaker brother. Indeed, it would be **well** and proper **not to eat meat nor to drink wine** nor in fact to **do anything** which would cause one's weaker comrade in Christ to **stumble** and fall from the Lord. Meat and wine are the normal components of feasting, yet the stronger brother must be willing to avoid these also when the weaker brother is present, if the only alternative is to do him harm.

Thus, ***the* faith** and convictions concerning these things which the stronger brother has, let him have **according to** him**self before God**, keeping such convictions in his own private way. He need not surrender his convictions about such things as food, but neither need he use them as weapons to beat another. Such peaceful eating and drinking and concern for the other are indeed **blessed** and are truly the way in which the blessing of God will rest upon their fellowship together. Then the stronger brother need not **judge** and condemn himself in eating **what he approves** at these feasts, for his eating does his weaker brother no harm.

St. Paul here makes a play on words. By showing concern for his weaker brother, the stronger brother need not **judge** himself (Gr. *krino*). For if the weaker brother analyzes and **doubts** himself (Gr. *diakrino*) when he **eats**, he is **condemned** by it (Gr. *katakrino*), for his eating is not **out of faith**. Thus, doubts here lead to condemnation for the weak and judgment on the strong. Let all avoid this judgment!

In saying that the weaker brother is condemned when he eats because his eating is not from faith, St. Paul means that this eating violates his faith in the Lord, expressing rejection of loyalty to Him. All such rejections of faith are **sin**. What is in view here is not a casual forgetting to give thanks before a meal. Rather, the apostle is thinking of one whose eating constitutes a crisis of faith and conscience. In saying that **all that is not out of faith is sin**, St. Paul is not stating a general principle, but reflecting on a specific situation. The apostle is saying that one incurs **sin** and guilt when he eats what he deeply feels is forbidden and thereby violates his inner commitment to Christ. It is the faithlessness of active rejection of Christ, rather than that of simply not believing in Him, which is in view.

15 1 **Now we who are powerful ought to bear the weakness of the ones who are not-powerful and not to please ourselves.**
2 **Let each of us please the neighbor for *his* good, to his building up.**
3 **For even the Christ did not please Himself, but as it is written, "The reproaches of those reproaching You fell on Me."**
4 **For whatever was written-before was written for our teaching, that through perseverance and through the encouragement of the Scriptures we might have the hope.**

The apostle now concludes his exhortation to the mixed community. Those **who are powerful** and strong in their faith **ought to bear the weakness of the ones** who are not. They should not merely think of how to **please** them**selves** by eating what they consider clean, but be willing to limit that liberty, **pleasing** their neighbor by respecting his conscience, **for *his* good**. The goal is **building up** the neighbor, not proving oneself right. (The urgency of the obligation is stressed by the verb *ought* being placed at the head of the sentence in the Greek.)

This necessity for self-sacrifice is emphasized by appeal to the example of **the Christ** Himself, who endured injustice for the sake of righteousness. St. Paul cites Psalm 69:9, which he interprets messianically. In its original context, this psalm was a cry of distress, the lament of one persecuted and misunderstood. David says that he is being persecuted for his piety, and that those who oppose and reproach God also oppose and reproach him for being His servant, so that **the reproaches of those reproaching** God could be said to fall on him. As a prophecy of the Davidic Messiah (He whose zeal consumes Him; see Ps. 69:9a; John 2:17), this passage speaks of how Christ bore the brunt of persecution from those who misunderstood and opposed His divine mission, enduring suffering in order to save the world.

The apostle cites this passage because it shows how one should sacrifice one's own desires and forgo pleasing oneself in order to further the salvation of others. If Christ sacrificed His life and endured such fearful reproaches and suffering for the sake of these our brothers, should we also not sacrifice some of our liberty to help them?

In thus quoting the Scriptures (literally "the Writings," Gr. *ton Graphon*), St. Paul reminds us that all that was **written-before** (Gr. *proegraphe*) was **written** (Gr. *egraphe*) for **our teaching**. That is, the ancient Writings of Israel prophesy our own Christian movement, and these things were written in advance for the later guidance of the Christians. In thus deriving lessons from the Psalter on how to live together as a church, St. Paul is simply using those writings according to their original intent (see 1 Cor. 10:11).

5 Now may the God of perseverance and encouragement give you the same mind among one another according to Christ Jesus,
6 that with the same-impulse, with one mouth, you may glorify the God and Father of our Lord Jesus Christ.

St. Paul then offers a prayer, that **the God of perseverance and encouragement** might grant them to be of **the same mind** and focus (Gr. *phroneo*, see 8:5) as they live **among one another** as a church **according to Christ Jesus**. If in their common life together they follow the Lord's example of self-sacrifice and have harmony among themselves, then they can **glorify God** with a truly united worship. If they can receive this gift of harmony from God, then they can offer their liturgical praise **with the same-impulse** and united heart (Gr. *omothumadon*, see its use in Acts 1:14; 2:46; 4:24) and **with one mouth**. Then their worship will ascend to God as if it came from a single heart and a single voice. Only then can they truly **glorify God**—for such glorification of God is only possible if their worship comes from a truly united and harmonious community.

Their God is the God who gives **perseverance and encouragement** to His People, and this is how He gives it—by granting them harmony together as a community. Let them receive this gift and be enabled to persevere and be encouraged.

7 Therefore, take in one another as the Christ also took you in, to *the* glory of God.
8 For I say, Christ has become a servant of *the* circumcision for *the* truth of God so as to confirm the promises of the Fathers,
9 but so that the Gentiles might glorify God for mercy, as it is written, "Therefore I will confess to You among the Gentiles and I will sing to Your Name."
10 And again He says, "Be glad, O Gentiles, with His People!"
11 And again, "Praise the Lord, all the Gentiles, and let all the peoples praise Him!"
12 And again Isaiah says, "There shall be the Root of Jesse, even He who rises to rule Gentiles; on Him Gentiles will hope."
13 Now *may* the God of the hope fill you with all joy and peace in having faith that you *yourselves* may abound in the hope by *the* power of *the* Holy Spirit.

St. Paul concludes by repeating his original directive to **take in one another** (14:1), even as **the Christ also took you in, to the glory of God**. Christ showed the fullness of the divine generosity in gathering to Himself and accepting all of them, regardless of their race, regardless of their opinions, regardless of their sins. Welcoming them all just as they were, He bestowed upon them the forgiveness of sins and His transfiguring grace. In the same way, they must welcome and accept one another, with the same openness and generosity as Christ has showed them. For just as their forgiveness and transfiguration by Christ redound to ***the*** **glory of God**, so will their mutual acceptance by one another redound to His glory.

The apostle emphasizes, beginning his sentence with **I say**, that Christ includes both Jews and Gentiles in the same saving embrace. He has become God's **servant** (Gr. *diakonos*) to the Jewish **circumcision**, **confirm**ing God's **promises** to **the Fathers** and vindicating God's **truth** and faithfulness to His covenant. God promised Israel that He would save them, and in Christ He has done so.

But He has come to save the Gentiles too, to whom He made no promises. They have no right to salvation, nor to expect that the God of Israel will be good to them—especially after their persecution of Israel! Nonetheless, in Christ, God has **mercy** on them as well, so that they might **glorify** Him for such unexpected kindness.

This generous inclusion of the Gentiles along with Israel—which outraged all the religious and social conventions of that day—was foretold by the Prophets. The mixed community in Rome should live together in peace, as their situation is the fulfillment of the ancient hope of the Scriptures. It is **as it is written** in Psalm 18:49: **"I will confess to You among the Gentiles and I will sing to Your Name."**

Here David pictures himself as confessing the mighty works of the Lord, surrounded by those from many nations who have come to join him in giving thanks to the Hebrew God. This is seen as a prophetic foreshadowing of the Gospel day enjoyed by Paul's readers, when Gentile and Jew would join together in confessing God's grace and singing to His Name.

Again in Deuteronomy 32:43, the Scripture writes prophetically of the nations flocking to acknowledge the power of Israel's God, saying, "**Be glad, O Gentiles** [or *nations*, Gr. *ethne*], **with His People!**" Here also, at the very beginning of the Jewish and Mosaic dispensation, this joint assembly of Gentiles with Jews is celebrated and foretold.

Yet **again** this unheard-of wonder is revealed. Psalm 117 foretells how the "truth of the Lord" and His covenant faithfulness remain to the ages (Ps. 117:2; see Rom. 15:8), drawing **all the Gentiles** and nations to Him, causing them to **praise** and worship Him (Ps. 117:1). Here again, the Gentiles are included along with the covenant people of Israel, praising the Hebrew God with one voice.

This theme of God's free mercy to the Gentiles of the earth is prophesied by the great **Isaiah** (11:10) when he says, "**There shall be the Root of Jesse**" (the Messiah from the line of David the son of Jesse) who shall **rise** in Israel **to rule** even over **Gentiles**. And this ruling does not involve the lowly subjugation of the Gentiles, as if they were made mere slaves to Israel. Rather, **on Him** those **Gentiles will hope**, looking to Him for rescue, security, and life, even as Israel does.

Thus, all the Scriptures are clear—from Moses to David to Isaiah—and glow with the radiant **hope** of universal, interracial salvation that they now enjoy. If such an harmonious combination of Jew with Gentile is the theme of so much of the Scriptures, how can they not rejoice in it and preserve that harmony?

St. Paul concludes with a prayer, that he might seal his exhortation with a blessing. He prays that **the God of the hope**—even that messianic hope of final salvation to which they are all bound—might **fill you with all joy and peace** as they have **faith**. If they can receive this gift of **joy and peace**, they will easily leave all quarreling behind. Then they can **abound** and overflow in that prophesied messianic **hope**, putting down the fleshly practices of the body **by *the* power of *the* Holy Spirit** (see 8:13). Then their lives will not be weighed down by their sufferings, but be made buoyant by the certainty of their coming salvation.

For their God is the God who gives hope and who bestows the serenity of certainty and lightness of heart. And this is *how* He gives it and causes it to **abound** in them—by empowering them to live together in peace and to have joy in each other. As they live their life of faith in such harmony together, the Holy Spirit can cause that hope to reign untroubled among them.

Notes for Section V:

Notes for Section V:

VI

CONCLUSION
(15:14—16:27)

§VI.1 St. Paul's plan to visit Rome

After his extended admonition and instruction to the Roman church (1:16—15:13), St. Paul finally returns to his plans for his proposed upcoming visit.

15 14 **And I have been persuaded, my brothers, even I myself, concerning you, that you yourselves are full of goodness, filled with all knowledge, able also to admonish one another.**
15 **But I have written daringly to you in part, as reminding you, because of the grace given me from God,**
16 **that I *might* be Christ Jesus' offerer to the Gentiles, serving-as-priest the Gospel of God, that my oblation of the Gentiles may be well-accepted, sanctified by *the* Holy Spirit.**
17 **I have therefore *my* boasting in Christ Jesus in things pertaining to God.**

He begins by declaring that such a long admonition is not to be taken as an indication that the apostle considers the Romans unruly, untaught, or stupid. Far from it, he hastens to assure them! He has been **persuaded**, he says emphatically (the **I, myself** is emphatic in the Greek), that he can have full confidence in them. He tenderly calls them his **brothers** and says he has no fears that they are unruly or wicked, but rather knows they are **full of goodness**. He does not regard them as untaught, slow beginners, but as **filled with all knowledge, able also to admonish** and warn **one another**.

Diplomatically, St. Paul says that he has only **written** to them so **daringly** on some things (**in part**) by way of **reminding** them of what they doubtless already know, so that it might be ever fresh in their minds. That is, he says, his task as an apostle. As a true apostle (here he gently moves to the fore his apostolic authority), he has been given **grace from God** that he might be **Christ Jesus' offerer to the Gentiles**.

Here he uses an extended metaphor of priestly sacrifice, drawn possibly from Isaiah 66:20. Isaiah prophesies of the Kingdom of God as a time when the Israelites returning from exile will "bring their brothers from all the nations as a gift to the Lord." In this prophecy, those of postexilic Israel offer to God their Jewish brothers who return from the Diaspora as a kind of living offering upon their return to Jerusalem.

In like manner, St. Paul sees his apostolic ministry as that of being **Christ Jesus'** priestly **offerer** (Gr. *leitourgos*, one who serves *leitourgia* or cultic sacrifice). It is his task to **serve-as-priest the Gospel of God**. (The term translated here *serve-as-priest* is the Gr. *ierourgeo*, cognate with the word *iereus* or "priest.") The thought contained in the metaphor is that even as the Levitical priests serve the Mosaic Law, so he serves **the Gospel** (see 4 Macc. 7:8, which speaks of the priest as "serving-as-priest the Law of God"). As sacrificial offerers, the Levitical priests offer the blood of animals. As the Lord's **offerer**, St. Paul offers the **oblation** (Gr. *prosphora*) **of the Gentiles**. And as the Levitical priests take care that their sacrificial oblations are pure and unblemished, so St. Paul takes care that his own living oblations, consisting of his Gentile converts, are also **well-accepted** by God, having been **sanctified by *the* Holy Spirit**.

Thus, his **boasting** and that for which he can expect a reward is **in things pertaining to God**—that is, the things of priestly cultic sacrifice. St. Paul means that his apostolic ministry is considered by him as a kind of priesthood. The Gentiles whom he has converted to Christ are his sacrifice to God, and, as a true **offerer** making an **oblation**, he must take pains that he is offering only the very best. That is why, he insists, he has written to them such a daring admonition and such a long letter. He is only doing his job as priest, making sure that his sacrifice of their lives to the Lord is **sanctified by *the* Holy Spirit**.

18 For I will not dare to speak of anything except what Christ has worked out through me, to the obedience of *the* Gentiles, by word and work,
19 in *the* power of signs and wonders, in *the* power of *the* Spirit of God, so that from Jerusalem and as far around as Illyricum, I have fulfilled the Gospel of Christ.
20 And thus I had as my ambition to preach *the Gospel* not where Christ was named, that I might not build on another's foundation,
21 but, as it is written, "Those to whom it was not announced about Him will see, and those who have not heard shall have insight."

The apostle stresses that his boasting is not based on any merit or private accomplishments of his own. His own circumcision and Jewish identity count here for nothing. Rather, his boasting and hope of reward are only in his sacrificial ministry to Christ—in **what Christ has worked out** through him, producing **the obedience of *the* Gentiles**. *That* is his ground for boasting and of that only does he **dare to speak**. Through both his **word and work**, through both his insightful preaching of the Mystery of the Gospel and his miraculous works of healing, he has **fulfilled the Gospel of Christ**. Wherever he has gone throughout the wide world, **from Jerusalem** as the center **as far round as** the borders of distant **Illyricum** (the area opposite Italy, on the east shore of the Adriatic), he has preached with attesting **signs and wonders**, manifesting the power of ***the*** **Spirit of God** through the conversion of many Gentiles. He has indeed **fulfilled** the preaching of ***the Gospel***, by obediently proclaiming what was given him to proclaim. Nonetheless, the stress here is not on what *Paul* has done, but on what *Christ* has done *through Paul*.

In all of his apostolic labors, he underscores, his **ambition** has been to go ever further afield. He has not been content simply to teach Christians who have been converted by someone else. That is a worthy task, but it is not the task given to him. His own special mandate is to **preach *the Gospel* not where Christ** is already **named**—for that would be to **build on another's foundation**. His task as apostle is to proclaim the Gospel to those who have never heard it before, to make brand-new converts. The prophecy of God's Suffering Servant in Isaiah 52:15 speaks of "**those to whom it was not announced**" as **seeing** what God has done, and of those who have never before **heard** of it as receiving **insight**. This messianic prophecy, Paul says, is fulfilled in his own apostolic work. His going ever further afield—eventually, he hopes, to Rome and then to Spain—is a part of this divine plan for the salvation of the world.

22 Therefore also I have often been hindered greatly in coming to you,
23 but now, with no longer place in these regions, and since I have had a desire for many years to come to you,
24 whenever I proceed to Spain, for I hope to see you *while* proceeding-through and to be sent forth by you from there, when first I have been filled in part.

That is why, St. Paul assures the Romans, he has not visited them before (see 1:10). His detractors may have suggested that he has not come to Rome before because he has no real interest in them. On the contrary, says the apostle, he has **had a desire for many years** and has **often** tried to visit Rome, but has been **hindered greatly** in coming there by his many other journeys and apostolic obligations. But **now** he has fulfilled all these, and he has **no longer place in** those **regions** where he is. Nothing now prevents him from fulfilling the long desire of his heart and coming to them. Indeed, he intends to **proceed to Spain**, the remotest western part of the Roman world (the trip from Rome to Spain was a journey of between 1000 and 1700 miles, depending upon the route). He is hoping to **proceed-through** Rome and be **sent forth** to Spain by them. That is, he proposes that he sojourn in Rome with them for a while and that they then help fund his trip further west—after, of course, he has **first been filled in part** (that is, after he has enjoyed their company for a while).

25 **But now, I am proceeding to Jerusalem serving the saints.**
26 **For Macedonia and Achaia were well-pleased to make some sharing for the poor among the saints in Jerusalem.**
27 **For they were well-pleased and were debtors to them, for if the Gentiles have shared in their spiritual things, they are debtors to them also to offer to them the fleshly things.**
28 **Therefore, when I have completed this and sealed this fruit to them, I will go through you to Spain,**
29 **and I know that when I come to you, I will come in the fullness of Christ's blessing.**

St. Paul wants to let the Romans know, however, that this visit will not be immediate. He first has to **proceed to Jerusalem**, fulfilling the charitable task of **serving the saints** there. (It is perhaps significant that the word *serving* is the Gr. *diakoneo*, cognate with the word for "deacon," whose task it was to tend to the poor; see Acts 6:1f.) The apostle has been collecting funds from all the churches in **Macedonia and Achaia** (he is writing from Achaia) for **the poor among the saints in Jerusalem**. This is the apostle's pet project, which is meant to unite Gentiles and Jews and to vindicate his Gentile mission. Just as the Jews of the Diaspora regularly sent money to Jerusalem for the support of the Temple and thereby proved themselves to be true Jews, so by this offering, the Gentile Christians will prove themselves to the Jewish Christians to be their true spiritual kin.

The Gentiles of these churches have made contributions earmarked for the poor in Jerusalem. Not only are they **well-pleased** to do so (St. Paul affirms this twice); they are also **debtors to them** and are morally obliged to do so. For if they make a **sharing** (Gr. *koinonia*) by offering those in Jerusalem **fleshly things** of money, they also first **shared** (Gr. *koinoneo*) **in their spiritual things** by receiving the Gospel from the apostles sent out from there.

St. Paul, therefore, is himself obliged to fulfill this important task, to **complete** it and **seal** that **fruit** to the church in Jerusalem. That is, he has first to proceed from Achaia to Jerusalem, delivering the **fruit** of the Greeks' generosity and certifying that this is all the money that was given, thereby setting his seal on the task as accomplished.

The word translated here *complete* is the Greek *epiteleo*, the technical word used for the completion of a sacrifice. By using this term, the apostle says that the money he is carrying is the Gentiles' spiritual sacrifice to God, and that they are offering it to God through him. St. Paul surely has to fulfill this worthy work first before he will be at liberty to visit Rome.

He will at length come to Rome, however, on the way **to Spain**. And, though they have to wait for his arrival, when he finally comes, he will come **in the fullness of Christ's blessing**. Once he has obediently accomplished his task in Jerusalem, the blessing of the Lord will rest upon him, and it is this blessing in all its fullness that he will be able to impart to them when he comes to Rome.

30 Now I exhort you, brothers, through our Lord
Jesus Christ and through the love of the Spirit,
that you co-contest with me in the prayers for
me to God,
31 that I may be rescued from the disobedient in
Judea and that my service for Jerusalem may
be well-accepted by the saints,
32 that having come to you in joy through *the* will
of God, I may be co-refreshed with you.

In typical humility, St. Paul speaks to the Romans tenderly as **brothers**, asking for their prayers. This is no mere literary convention or casual request—he really wants their prayers. He thus **exhorts** them **through our Lord Jesus Christ**, appealing to the fullness of his apostolic authority in the Church, and **through the love of the Spirit**, appealing to the love the Spirit places in the hearts of believers for all their fellow-believers. Appealing to both external authority and internal love, he urges that they **co-contest** with him in **the prayers** they offer **to God**.

The word translated here *co-contest* is the Greek *sunagonizomai*. It is related to the word *agonizomai*, which means "to engage in an athletic contest," such as a race (Gr. *agon*; see Heb. 12:1). By using this word, St. Paul means that he himself strives in prayer, straining and laboring as would an athlete in the games, and he wants them to strive in prayer also. Only then, he feels, will he be **rescued from the disobedient** Jews **in Judea** who oppose him, and only then will his **service** (Gr. *diakonia*) and offering for the Christian poor in Jerusalem be **well-accepted** by the church there.

In short, the apostle is greatly concerned about his trip to Jerusalem. Not only is he worried that the unbelieving Jews will find a way to stop him (as it turned out, not a groundless fear!—see Acts 21:27f), but he also fears that the church there will reject his offering of money from the Gentiles. Perhaps, he thinks, some Christians there who are zealous for the Law (see Acts 21:20) will not accept the gift precisely because it comes through him, and they want nothing to do with anything sent from the uncircumcised. His journey to Jerusalem, therefore, is still a source of concern for him.

That is why he covets their prayers. He hopes that after all his work in Jerusalem is done, through their prayers and **through *the* will of God** he will come safely and **in joy** to Rome. Then he will be **co-refreshed** with them.

The word translated *co-refreshed* is the Greek *sunanapauomai.* It is related to the word *anapauo,* which means "to stop and rest and be refreshed" (see its use in Matt. 11:28 for the rest that the Lord gives to the weary soul). By using the related *sunanapauomai* here, St. Paul means to express that he trusts that both he and they will find restful refreshment through his visit to them. His trip to Rome may have to wait for yet a little while longer, but it will be worth the wait!

33 Now the God of the peace *be* with you all. Amen.

The apostle comes at last to the conclusion of his epistle. As was customary in those days, he ends his epistle with a blessing, asking **God** that He might abide among them and bestow the gift of **peace** they have come to know. This peace is not simply the absence of strife—it is the abundance of harmony and spiritual well-being that only comes through experiencing God's Presence. St. Paul prays that God might dwell among them in His fullness, and this is to be their peace.

§VI.2 Final greetings

St. Paul adds final greetings, as was common in epistles in those days, greeting those he knows who are then in Rome.

The apostle's general policy was not to greet individuals by name at the end of his epistles. Perhaps this policy was motivated by Paul's desire to avoid the appearance of favoritism. In communities where he had visited personally and where he had formed relationships with the rank and file, he was reluctant to single out individuals, lest he give offense to those in the community who were not mentioned. But in the Roman community, where he had never visited and where he knew none of the local rank and file, this was not an issue. He therefore sends greetings to those friends of his whom he knows from elsewhere and who are then sojourning in Rome. Some have thought it odd that Paul would know so many people in Rome, since he had never been there. But in those days, all roads did indeed lead to Rome, and travel to the great center was relatively easy. It was by no means unlikely that so many of his friends might then be visiting Rome.

Beyond this merely historical interest, the presence of so many names here has an abiding theological significance. It reveals the importance of relationship in the Christian Faith. Discipleship to Christ does not involve only nurturing one's relationship to the Lord—it involves also nurturing one's relationships to one's brothers and sisters.

16 1 **I commend to you our sister Phoebe, who is a servant of the church in Cenchrea;**
2 **and that you welcome her in *the* Lord, *in a manner* worthy of the saints, and that you stand-by her in whatever matter she may have need, for indeed she has been a presider of many and of myself.**

St. Paul begins by **commending** his **sister** in Christ **Phoebe**, from **the church in Cenchrea**, the port of nearby Corinth whence Paul is writing. Such commendation is perhaps especially needed since women were not usually held in high regard in that culture, and Phoebe would be required, as the bearer of the letter, to explain to the church there anything in the letter they did not understand. Thus the apostle urges them to **welcome her** ***in a manner*** **worthy** of their calling to be **saints.** That is, they are to **stand-by her in whatever matter she may have need**, coming to her side to provide whatever she might require.

Phoebe's qualifications are given: she is a **servant** (Gr. *diakonos*) of the church and further has been **a presider of many**, including Paul himself.

Despite the use of the word *diakonos* to describe Phoebe, it is unlikely that Paul means that she functions as a deacon. Though the word is used with this technical meaning in Philippians 1:1 and 1 Timothy 3:8, St. Paul usually uses it in a nontechnical sense, to denote any "servant." Thus Paul describes himself as a *diakonos* (Col. 1:23), as well as his fellow-worker Tychicus (Eph. 6:21) and even Christ Himself (15:8). Furthermore, Church history knows nothing more of women deacons until about the early third century. If Phoebe were an actual woman deacon, the absence of the order of women deacons or deaconesses from the first to the third century would be difficult to account for. It would seem that Phoebe is a "servant" of the church in Cenchrea in that she functions as a patroness of that church, probably opening her home to the church and hosting its gatherings. She is evidently a woman of some wealth, which would explain why she is delegated to carry Paul's letter to Rome.

This would seem to be the meaning of her being described as a *presider* of the church there (Gr. *prostatis*, from the verb *proistemi*, meaning "to stand before, administrate, manage"). A *prostates* (a masculine noun) is one who manages, helps, facilitates, and does the work of administration. The term is used by St. Paul to describe the church's presbyters, whose job it is to rule and manage the church (12:8; 1 Thess. 5:12). A *prostatis* would be a feminine manager. Does this mean that Phoebe functions as a presbyter?

That is unlikely, given St. Paul's other strictures regarding women (e.g. 1 Cor. 14:34). Rather, the title *prostatis* seems to be given as an honorary title to those women who help the church financially and socially as patrons. It would thus be on par with the Jewish practice of honoring rich benefactors of the synagogue with the honorary title *archisynagogos*, which, though used to describe a position of real authority when held by a man, carried no such real authority when bestowed honorifically upon a woman. It is in this honorary sense that Phoebe is described as a *presider* or administrator of the church, for in her capacity as patron, she has been a helper of many and of St. Paul himself.

3 Greet Prisca and Aquila my coworkers in Christ Jesus,
4 who for my soul laid-down their own necks, to whom not only do I myself *give* thanksgiving, but also all the churches of the Gentiles.
5 Also *greet* the church that is in their house. Greet Epaenetus my beloved, who is the first-fruit of Asia for Christ.

St. Paul also asks the Romans to greet **Prisca and Aquila**, his **coworkers in Christ Jesus**. These two are a husband-and-wife team who travel much, sharing the Gospel and instructing converts (see Acts 18:26). Being Jewish, they were expelled from Rome when Emperor Claudius ordered all the Jews to leave Rome (Acts 18:2), and they found St. Paul in Corinth. Evidently, since the imperial edict has been relaxed somewhat, they have returned to Rome and are there when the apostle writes from Corinth.

Of the two, it would seem that Prisca is the more prominent, since her name is often mentioned before that of her husband (see Acts 18:18, 26; 2 Tim. 4:19), possibly a sign of her superior social standing. These two have **laid-down their necks** for the apostle's **soul** or life—that is, they have risked their own safety in order to help him, so that Paul gives **thanksgiving** to God for them—as do **all the churches of the Gentiles** whom the apostle has told of their courage. The Christians of Rome are to pass on the apostle's warmest greetings to his old friends—and also to **the church** that meets **in their house** there. Evidently, Priscilla and Aquila are continuing their practice of gathering and teaching the Christians!

St. Paul gives quick greetings to others as well. **Epaenetus** receives greetings as Paul's **beloved** friend—all the more so, perhaps, because he was Paul's **first-fruit** or convert **for Christ** in the province of **Asia** Minor. The name was common to slaves (though not confined to them). Perhaps Epaenetus is a freed slave, converted by Apollos in Ephesus (see Acts 19:1f).

6 Greet Mary who has toiled much for you.

Other greetings follow in quick succession. They are to greet **Mary**, who **has toiled much for you**. Maria could be a Latin *nomen*, one of several names carried by those of higher rank, possibly indicating that she is a citizen. If that is so, she would be a woman of some importance and her **toil** could well consist in organizing the church there and possibly functioning as a patron.

7 Greet Andronicus and Junia, my kinsmen and my fellow-captives, who are notable among the apostles, who were also in Christ before me.

They are to greet **Andronicus and Junia**, evidently another couple, described by the apostle as his **kinsmen** (probably meaning that they are Jews; see the use of the term in 9:3) and as his **fellow-captives**. We do not know to which time in prison St. Paul here refers. He elsewhere writes that he had abundant imprisonments (2 Cor. 11:23), and it could refer to any of these. It would seem that they either shared this time in prison with St. Paul or else visited him while he was in prison so often that they could be dryly described as **fellow-captives** themselves.

They are further described as being **in Christ before** St. Paul (that is, they were converted before he was), and as being **notable**

among the apostles. This could mean that the apostles consider them to be notable, but it is more likely that St. Paul means that they are both **apostles** themselves, and **notable** ones at that.

By **apostle**, St. Paul does not of course mean that they are among the Twelve. The term *apostolos* means "one sent out, an ambassador" and can be used to describe anyone sent out as a messenger (see Phil. 2:25). It is in this sense that the Seventy are referred to as "apostles" (see Luke 10:1). It is possible that Andronicus is one of those Seventy, now ministering with his wife Junia, who here shares with her husband the dignity of the apostolic title.

(Note: Despite the fact that some take the Greek *Jounian* here to be the accusative of the masculine name Junias and thus try to make this woman into a man, it is clear that St. Paul refers to a woman, Junia. The masculine name Junias [or its longer form Junianus] is not attested at all in any Greek document.)

8 Greet Ampliatus, my beloved in *the* Lord.
9 Greet Urbanus our coworker in Christ, and
Stachys my beloved.

Greetings are also sent to **Ampliatus** and to **Stachys**, St. Paul's **beloved** friends, and to **Urbanus**, a **coworker** with Paul and his fellow apostles, and one who evidently shares their apostolic labors. The names Ampliatus and Urbanus were common Roman slave names, and perhaps these are freedmen.

10 Greet Apelles, the approved in Christ. Greet
those who are of the *house* of Aristobulus.
11 Greet Herodion, my kinsman. Greet those of
the *house* of Narcissus, who are in *the* Lord.

Greetings are sent to **Apelles**, whom St. Paul praises as **the approved in Christ**, no doubt for this proven perseverance under difficult circumstances.

Next follow greetings to those slaves or freedmen from the households of **Aristobulus** and **Narcissus**. It is possible that these two men are to be identified with their famous namesakes. Aristobulus was the grandson of Herod the Great and was educated and brought up in Rome. Upon his death, it is not unlikely that his household would pass to his friend, the Emperor Claudius, though still retaining the name of their former master. Narcissus was a freedman and a favorite of the emperor, who died shortly before St. Paul wrote this epistle. His household also could well have passed to Claudius while still retaining his name.

If these guesses are correct, the church in Rome has begun to make important contacts, and possibly that is why these are singled out by the apostle for special greetings. But it is possible that other men are meant. Certainly Aristobulus was not an uncommon name.

St. Paul sends greetings to **Herodion**, described as Paul's **kinsman**—that is, a fellow Jew. His name suggests some connection with the household of Herod.

12 Greet Tryphaena and Tryphosa, laborers in *the* Lord. Greet Persis the beloved, who has labored much in *the* Lord.

Next the apostle sends greetings to three women. He greets **Tryphaena and Tryphosa** (probably sisters), who were **laborers** for the Lord, busy with charitable works in the church. He also greets **Persis**, whom he describes as **the beloved**—*not*, we note, as "*my* beloved," because it would be indelicate for him to describe a woman as his beloved. The apostle was careful to preserve modesty and to avoid even the appearance of any impropriety.

13 Greet Rufus, a chosen *man* in *the* Lord; also his mother and mine.

St. Paul also sends greetings to **Rufus** and his **mother**. This is possibly the same Rufus referred to in Mark 15:21, whose father was Simon of Cyrene, the one who helped the Lord carry His Cross. Since Mark's Gospel was written in Rome, this is not unlikely. Mark would then have mentioned Rufus in his narrative because he was a member of the church there. Whatever the truth of this guess, St. Paul sends Rufus his greeting as to one **chosen** and prominent in the church, along with his mother, who had befriended Paul also with her maternal care.

14 Greet Asyncritus, Phlegon, Hermes, Patrobas, Hermas, and the brothers with them.

Then follows a series of names, some of which (**Phlegon, Hermes, Hermas**) were commonly borne by slaves. Little can be said for certain of these, though a fertile tradition later makes them apostles and bishops (feast day April 8).

15 Greet Philologus and Julia, Nereus and his sister and Olympas, and all the saints with them.

The same uncertainty attaches itself to these names. **Julia** was a common slave name, but it was also a *nomen*, and could indicate a Roman citizen. It would seem that perhaps **Philologus and Julia** were brother and sister. The reference to **all the saints with them** may indicate that these all together formed a kind of community or house-church.

16 Greet one another with a holy kiss. All the churches of Christ greet you.

Lastly in his greetings, St. Paul asks them to **greet one another** when they have come together and read his epistle, sealing their fellowship with the **holy kiss.** This liturgical kiss is the sign of unity with which their prayers culminate and it is exchanged between **one another**, regardless of gender. Later on, as the church grew, this kiss would have to become more regulated for the sake of propriety and it would be exchanged only within the genders, with men greeting men and women greeting women. But during this time of closeness and smaller numbers, the church was a more intimate assembly, and it was exchanged between all.

As they greet one another at Paul's request, he sends greetings from **all the churches of Christ** where he has visited. For no church community exists in isolation. If it is to be healthy, it must cherish unity between all and have its heart open to the world.

§VI.3 Appeal for peace

17 Now I exhort you, brothers, watch out for those doing the dissensions and the stumbling-blocks, against the teaching you learned, and turn away from them.

18 For such serve *as slaves*, not of our Lord Jesus Christ, but of their own belly, and by their kind-words and blessing deceive the hearts of the guileless.

19 For your obedience has reached to all; therefore I rejoice concerning you, but I want you to be wise in what is good and innocent in what is wicked.

20 And the God of the peace will break Satan under your feet quickly. The grace of our Lord Jesus *be* with you!

St. Paul now adds an exhortation to unity, earnestly warning the Roman faithful against those creating **the dissensions and the**

stumbling-blocks and disturbing the peace. Some have thought that this warning against sowers of dissension comes rather abruptly, placed as it is in the middle of final greetings. But such abrupt tangents are typical of St. Paul's spirited style of dictation. In his Epistle to the Philippians, for example, it seems as if he were going to begin his conclusion by saying, "Rejoice in the Lord" (Phil. 3:1; see 4:4), when he suddenly launches into a similar warning against the Judaizers. So it is here. As he thinks of all in the Roman community to whom he wants to send greetings, he seems to be thinking also of the possibility of those Judaizing troublemakers coming in among them and stirring up trouble. Indeed, it is to secure his reputation against their slanders that he is writing the epistle in the first place. So, whether he has just received reports of their wicked work among the Romans or whether he is writing to forearm the faithful against such work, St. Paul adds a few words, urging the faithful to preserve the peace that exists among them.

They have **learned** as true disciples **the teaching** of the apostolic Gospel (see 6:17), with its emphasis on the free grace of God. In their original Gospel catechesis, they were taught the truth. If any, therefore, should come among them or if any from within their own ranks should contradict that original deposit of the Faith, making **dissensions** and setting up **stumbling-blocks**, they must **turn away from them**. They already have the truth, and all have accepted it. Anyone who disturbs this peaceful status quo by arguing against the doctrine they have received does not serve the **Lord Jesus Christ**.

Rather, they **serve *as slaves*** their own **belly** and appetite. They might ply the faithful with many **kind-words** (Gr. *chrestologia*) and sweet-talking; they might pronounce many a **blessing** and tell them how spiritual they must be to accept all of their teaching. But they are not truly zealous for the Lord, even though they claim to be so. Rather, they are zealous for their own egos, and all their talk is simply a con trick to **deceive the hearts of the guileless** and unsuspecting. Let them **watch out** for such as these!

For it would be a shame to ruin such a good record as they have. Indeed, news of their **obedience** and faith has **reached to all**. All the world, wherever Paul has gone, has been impressed by the

Christians of Rome (see 1:8), and for this, the apostle **rejoices**. He is not warning them, therefore, because he has doubts about them. Far from it! Rather, it is only that he wants them **to be wise in what is good and innocent in what is wicked**. He only wants them to continue in their obedient faith and avoid future possible snares. If they will do that, staying far away from false teachers and treasuring their harmony and solidarity, then **the God** who gives His **peace** to His people will come to their aid and will **break Satan under** their **feet quickly**. Satan's plan is to sow dissension among them, to put obstacles in their path to trip them up and impede their progress to the Kingdom. But their solidarity will shut him out and overthrow him. Even as the righteous are given to tread upon the serpentine dragon (Ps. 91:13), so will the God of peace and victory cause them to crush underfoot their ancient foe.

After this warning, the apostle comes to his conclusion. Since it is his practice to add the last few words in his own handwriting (see 2 Thess. 3:17), it is possible that he adds the final and customary apostolic benediction with his own hand, saying, **The grace of our Lord Jesus be with you!**

21 **Timothy my coworker greets you; *as do* Lucius and Jason and Sosipater, my kinsmen.**
22 **I *myself*, Tertius, the one having written the epistle, greet you in *the* Lord.**
23 **Gaius, host *of strangers* for me and for the whole church, greets you. Erastus, the steward of the city, greets you, *as does* also Quartus, the brother.**

At the epistle's conclusion, those staying with Paul add their own greetings, wishing to be remembered by the Christians of Rome. **Timothy** his **coworker** was often with him and was thus included by Paul in his greetings (see 1 Thess. 1:1).

Paul's **kinsmen** and fellow-Jews are harder to identify with any certainty. **Lucius** could be the teacher alluded to in Acts 13:1. **Jason** could be the one who welcomed St. Paul when he was in Thessalonica (Acts 17:5), though he is not mentioned in Acts 20:4 along with the other Thessalonians who accompanied the apostle to Jerusalem. **Sosipater** could be the Sopater of Berea listed in Acts 20:4. But these names were not uncommon in antiquity.

As the apostle is dictating these greetings, his amanuensis and scribe **Tertius** seems to have spoken up and asked leave to add his own greetings in the first person, which St. Paul graciously allows. Very often scribes were literate slaves, and perhaps here was a case of Gaius, Paul's host, offering him the use of his own slave to act as scribe. Whatever the particulars, Tertius was also a believer, and adds his own words to the apostle's.

After the enthusiastic interruption of his scribe, St. Paul returns to dictation, passing on the greetings of his host, **Gaius**. The word translated here *host of strangers* is the Greek *xenos*, often translated "stranger" (e.g. Acts 17:21). Gaius was not simply the apostle's host, putting him up in his home; he was **host of strangers** for **the whole church** as well, opening his home to any Christians who were passing through and required lodging. Though the name Gaius was a common one, he would appear to be the same man mentioned in 1 Cor. 1:14, whom the apostle baptized along with Crispus.

As well as passing on the greetings of his affluent host, St. Paul passes on the greetings of another important Christian, **Erastus**, who was **steward** and treasurer of the city. Some identify him with the apostle's traveling companion mentioned in Acts 19:22, and also with the one who remained at Corinth (2 Tim. 4:20). Though one might expect that such an important civic official would have to stay resident in the city, it is possible that he was able to take some time to travel with the apostle. The identification, however, is not certain.

Finally, St. Paul passes on the greetings of **Quartus**. Nothing else is known of him for certain, other than that he is commended as **the brother**, or the Christian. It does reveal, however, the heart of the apostle, who generously included all in his work, however humble.

(It may be mentioned in passing that v. 24, **The grace of our Lord Jesus Christ be with you all. Amen**, is not present in the best manuscripts, and is not original to the epistle.)

§VI.4 Concluding blessing

25 **Now to the One who is able to establish you
according to my Gospel and the heralding of
Jesus Christ, according to *the* revelation of *the*
mystery which has been made silent for eternal times,**
26 **but now is manifested, and through the prophetic Scriptures, according to the command
of the eternal God, has been made known to
all the Gentiles, for *the* obedience of faith,**
27 **to the only wise God, through Jesus Christ, to
whom *be* the glory to the ages. Amen.**

At last St. Paul comes to his final words. Usually he concludes his epistles with a simple greeting, such as, "The grace of the Lord Jesus Christ be with your spirit" (e.g. Phil. 4:23). Here, however, where he feels the need to commend himself in preparation for his upcoming visit, he concludes with something more impressive and lengthy. It is as if, having finished his letter, the apostle takes a deep breath and utters one great, final, doctrinal cry of praise. Coming at the end of his letter (where most manuscripts contain it), it functions to crown all his previous words and drive home his qualifications to teach and be accepted as an apostle. (In giving the final blessing, St. Paul's ecstatic fervency and desire to teach seem to overcome concern for grammar, since, strictly speaking, the long sentence fragment lacks a predicate.)

He concludes by lifting up and exalting God as **the One who is able to establish** the believers according to the **Gospel** preached by St. Paul—the **heralding of Jesus Christ** to the nations. Implicit in this doxology is a statement of Paul's own apostolic authority—for, St. Paul says, the church was established by God according to **my Gospel.** Whatever his detractors might say, it is *his* Gospel that conveys the power of God (see 1:16). It is through it that men are **established** and made secure, able to withstand all the storms of life.

This Gospel is described as being **according to *the* revelation of *the* mystery** which has been kept **silent** and hidden **for eternal times**. That is, the Gospel of Jesus, the One who saves all men through their faith alone, is not some invention of Paul's. Rather, it is God's **mystery**, kept **silent** through the **eternal times** (Gr. *chronois aioniois*) of all human history up to that point, only now to be revealed to the initiated, the Christians. Before, no one had heard this Good News. But the time for that silence is over. **Now** it has been openly **manifested**. Appealing to **the prophetic Scriptures**, St. Paul and all the apostles have **made** it **known to all the Gentiles**.

By referring to *the prophetic Scriptures* (Gr. *Graphon prophetikon*), St. Paul does not mean just the writings of the Old Testament Prophets. Rather, he means that all the Old Testament **Scriptures** are in fact **prophetic** of that Gospel. The Law, the Prophets, the Psalms—all foretell this Gospel and confirm the **heralding** of the apostles.

This Gospel therefore is proclaimed by the apostles **to all the Gentiles** (Gr. *ethne*)—even to those in Rome (see 1:14, 15). This is not done from their own authority, as if they preached to advance their own ideas. On the contrary, Paul and the apostles preach in response to the **command of the eternal God**. *He* has sent them to preach to all the Gentiles, and Paul's imminent presence in Rome is the result of *God's* plan, not just Paul's own.

This is all to promote the **obedience of faith**. One last time, St. Paul asserts that salvation is not through conformity to the Jewish Law, but through faith. The Gentiles are saved as they put their faith in Christ, and strive to live as His obedient disciples.

Finally (taking another breath), the apostle comes again to lift up the God to whom **glory to the ages** is due **through Jesus Christ**. He is **the only wise God**. What is this wisdom, which He alone possesses? It is the plan of salvation—the astounding love that would cause Him to die for His enemies and thus transform them into His children and heirs, the unsearchable brilliance that could use the divisions between Jew and Gentile as the instrument to save both, the unfathomable mercy that shut up the whole world in a sinking solidarity of sin that it might have mercy upon all. This is their God, the God who has mercy and who saves. And it is His Gospel that Paul is called to bring to Rome—a single saving Gospel for all men.

Notes for Section VI:

Other books in *The Orthodox Bible Study Companion* Series:

- **The Prison Epistles:**
  Philippians, Ephesians, Colossians, Philemon
  224 pages—(ISBN 1-888212-52-7) $15.95
- **First and Second Corinthians: Straight from the Heart**
  319 pages—(ISBN 1-888212-53-5) $17.95
- **The Gospel of Mark: The Suffering Servant**
  224 pages—(ISBN 1-888212-54-2) $16.95
- **The Gospel of John: Beholding the Glory**
  376 pages—(ISBN 1-888212-55-1) $19.95

Other books available from Conciliar Press:

THE ORTHODOX STUDY BIBLE:
New Testament and Psalms

Genuine Leather Edition—$50.95; Hardcover Edition—$30.95;
Paperback Edition—$24.95

An edition of the New Testament and Psalms that offers Bible study aids written from an Orthodox perspective. Prepared under the direction of canonical Orthodox theologians and hierarchs, *The Orthodox Study Bible* presents a remarkable combination of historic theological insights and practical instruction in Christian living. *The Orthodox Study Bible* also provides a personal guide to help you apply biblical truths to your daily life with such excellent aids as: carefully prepared study notes on the text; a chart of Scripture readings to offer guidance for daily devotions; a guide for morning and evening prayers; readings for feast days; quotations from early Church fathers such as St. John Chrysostom, St. Ignatius of Antioch, St. Gregory of Nyssa, and St. Athanasius; a glossary of Orthodox Christian terminology; and the New King James Version translation with center-column cross references and translation notes.

CHRIST IN THE PSALMS

By Patrick Henry Reardon—$17.95

A highly inspirational book of meditations on the Psalms by one of the most insightful and challenging Orthodox writers of our day. Avoiding both syrupy sentimentality and arid scholasticism, *Christ in the Psalms* takes the reader on a thought-provoking and enlightening pilgrimage through this beloved "Prayer Book" of the Church.

Which psalms were quoted most frequently in the New Testament, and how were they interpreted? How has the Church historically understood and utilized the various psalms in her liturgical life? How can we perceive the image of Christ shining through the psalms? Lively and highly devotional, thought-provoking yet warm and practical, *Christ in the Psalms* sheds a world of insight upon each psalm, and offers practical advice for how to make the Psalter a part of our daily lives.

---

*Note: Prices listed were current as of May, 2006. Prices are subject to change. Prices do not include tax and postage & handling.

More books available from Conciliar Press:

JOURNEY TO THE KINGDOM: Reflections on the Sunday Gospels

By Fr. John Mack—$13.95

Reflections on selected Sunday Gospel readings by well-known priest and author, Father John Mack. Father John's insights into familiar Bible passages that we have often heard, but may not truly have understood, are excellent.

In 34 chapters, Father John takes us through the highlights of the church year and lovingly opens up the Gospel stories to us with patristic and biblical wisdom. Many of the reflections are filled with stories of the saints, as well as observations about living in the twenty-first century that lead us to ask deeper questions about our own lives.

Journey to the Kingdom deals with sin and grace, repentance and confession, living by faith, and many other needful topics. Perfect as a gift, for home use, or for group study.

SOLA SCRIPTURA: An Orthodox Analysis of the Cornerstone of Reformation Theology

By Fr. John Whiteford—$3.95

An Orthodox analysis of a Protestant bastion: private interpretation of Scripture. Exposes the fallacies on which this doctrine is based and explains the Orthodox approach to Holy Scripture. A 47-page booklet.

WHAT IS THE ORTHODOX CHURCH? A Brief Overview of Orthodoxy

by Fr. Marc Dunaway —$3.50

A brief overview of Orthodoxy. Outlines the history of the Christian Church, with concise explanations and helpful "at-a-glance" timelines. Includes the Age of Persecution, the Age of Councils, the Great Schism, the Protestant Reformation, and more. A 24-page booklet.

BECOMING ORTHODOX A Journey to the Ancient Christian Faith

by Fr. Peter E. Gillquist —$14.95

The inspiring story of over two thousand evangelical Christians and their search for historic Christianity. This book is for evangelical Christians on their own search for the Church. It is also for Orthodox Christians looking for renewal.

---

*Note: Prices listed were current as of May, 2006.
Prices are subject to change. Prices do not include tax and postage & handling.

To request a Conciliar Press catalog of other books
about the Orthodox Faith and church life,
to place a credit card order, or to obtain current ordering information,
please call Conciliar Press at (800) 967-7377 or (831) 336-5118,
or log on to our website: www.conciliarpress.com

Printed in the United States
211347BV00002B/23/A

9 781888 212518